Do
Brilliantly

A2 Psychology

Mike Cardwell and Cara Flanagan
Series Editor: Jayne de Courcy

Contents

How this book will help you 5

1 Social Psychology **13**

2 Physiological Psychology.....................**21**

3 Cognitive Psychology **28**

4 Developmental Psychology **35**

5 Comparative Psychology **42**

6 Perspectives: Individual Differences **49**

7 Perspectives: Issues **57**

8 Perspectives: Debates **66**

9 Perspectives: Approaches **75**

Answers to Questions to try **80**

Published by HarperCollinsPublishers Ltd
77–85 Fulham Palace Road
London W6 8JB

www.**Collins**Education.com
On-line support for schools and colleges

First published 2002

ISBN 0 00 712420 1

British Library Cataloguing in Publication Data
A catalogue record for this book is available from the British Library.

Edited by Brigitte Lee
Production by Kathryn Botterill
Book design by Gecko Ltd
Cover design by Susi Martin-Taylor
Printed and bound by Scotprint

Illustrations
Cartoon artwork Roger Penwill
DTP artwork Gecko Ltd

Every effort has been made to contact the holders of copyright material, but if any have been inadvertently overlooked, the Publishers will be pleased to make the necessary arrangements at the first opportunity.

You might also like to visit:
www.**fire**and**water**.com
The book lover's website

How this book will help you

by Mike Cardwell and Cara Flanagan

The topics covered by your AQA-A specification

This book will help you to improve your performance in the AQA (Specification A) A2 Psychology exam.

This exam consists of three units.

- **Unit 4 contains five sections:** social, physiological, cognitive, developmental and comparative psychology. Each section consists of three subsections and one question is set on each subsection. This results in a total of 15 questions. **You must answer three questions out of the total 15, taken from at least two sections.**

- **Unit 5 contains three sections:** individual differences, issues and debates, and approaches. **You must answer one question from each section.** There are three questions on individual differences, four questions on issues and debates (two on issues and two on debates), and two questions on approaches. This unit is special because it is assessed on 'synopticity', which is discussed further on page 12.

- **Unit 6 is the piece of coursework,** which does not involve a written examination.

The structure of this book

Section	Subsections	*Do Brilliantly* chapter number
Social psychology	Social cognition; Relationships; Pro- and anti-social behaviour	1
Physiological psychology	Brain and behaviour; Biological rhythms, Sleep and dreaming; Motivation and emotion	2
Cognitive psychology	Attention and pattern recognition; Perceptual processes and development; Language and thought	3
Developmental psychology	Cognitive development; Social and personality development; Adulthood	4
Comparative psychology	Determinants of animal behaviour; Animal cognition; Evolutionary explanations of human behaviour	5
Individual differences	Classification and diagnosis of psychological abnormality; Psychopathology; Treating mental disorders	6
Issues	Gender bias; Culture bias, Ethical issues; The use of non-human animals	7
Debates	Free will and determinism; Reductionism; Psychology as science; Nature–Nurture	8
Approaches	The question set tests knowledge about any two approaches in psychology, e.g. biological/medical, behavioural, psychodynamic and cognitive. [You may also use other approaches that are not part of the core specification, e.g. social constructionism, evolutionary psychology, sociology and philosophy.]	9

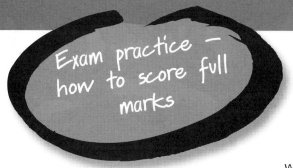
Exam practice –
how to score full
marks

Students frequently fail to perform as well as they might in exams because they have poor **exam skills** or cannot apply what they know effectively. This is evident from how surprised many students are when they receive an exam grade that bears little relation to the amount of work they have done in preparation for the exam.

To get a good grade in A2 level psychology you need to have a good grasp of the subject matter and good exam technique. Your main textbook will help you develop your knowledge and understanding. **This book can help you improve your exam technique, so that you can make the most effective use of what you know.**

There are nine chapters in this book, relating to the eight sections of the AQA Specification A A2 examination ('Issues' and 'Debates' are dealt with in two separate chapters). Each chapter is broken down into three separate elements:

① How to 'deconstruct' a question and plan an effective answer

Each chapter starts with three essay questions for that section of the specification, one from each of the subsections (see page 5). Each question is typical of the sort that you would find on a real AQA-A Unit 4 or Unit 5 paper. **We then select one of the questions and deconstruct it to show what special points you need to address when planning your response.** In particular we highlight the mark allocation for the question, focusing on the **AO1** and **AO2** demands (see page 8) and the meaning of specific terms (injunctions) (see page 9).

We provide a plan for the essay to show you how to produce a balanced response of an appropriate length, given both the time constraints of an exam and the demands of the question set. This is followed by a paragraph-by-paragraph breakdown of a possible response to the question.
We comment on the aims of each paragraph and list in bullet point format what might be contained in the paragraph.

② Student's answer, examiner's comments and 'How to score full marks'

For one of the exam questions, we provide a typical student answer. This answer highlights many of the **most common mistakes** that students make under exam conditions.

We provide a running commentary on the answer, noting the strengths and weaknesses of the essay.

This is followed by a **'How to score full marks'** section, making detailed comments on the essay. This information **should greatly help you in improving your essay-writing skills, resulting in higher marks and a better overall grade in your final exam**.

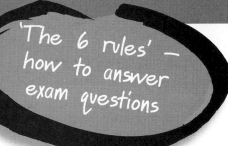

'The 6 rules' — how to answer exam questions

3 Question to try, Examiner's hints, Answer and Examiner's comments

Each chapter ends with an exam question for you to try answering. Examiner's hints are given which will help you focus on key points and give you ideas about what might be included in your essay.

The best way to answer the question is to do it as if you were in an exam. Try to remember all that you've read earlier in the chapter and put it into practice here. It is particularly important to time yourself and only write for the same length of time that you would have in the proper exam. It is best to find out now just what the time pressures are going to be like in the exam, and how this will affect the structure, appropriateness and coherence of your essay.

When you've written your answer, read it through and then turn to the back of the book. There you'll find an answer to the question that you've just done. This answer is an example of a very good 'A' grade response. **We've added our 'Examiner's comments' on it to show you exactly why it is such a good answer.**

Remember, there are no right answers in psychology, only well-informed ones. Don't feel you have to answer the question in the way suggested, but listen to the advice and adapt it for your own answer. If you feel your answer isn't as good as the one given, you can use the answer and the comments on it to give you ideas about where yours might be improved. You may find, for example, that you can incorporate sections of the model answer into your own answer.

Each of the AQA-A A2 written examinations will look like the sample below.

Each question on the exam is written to a set of rules. You will come to understand how these rules are applied as you work through the exemplar exam questions in this book. If you understand these rules, you will know better what to expect in the examination and how to answer the questions.

We go through each of the six rules briefly on pages 8–10.

Section C – Cognitive Psychology

7 Describe and evaluate **two or more** explanations of divided attention. [24 marks]

8 Discuss the structure and functions of the visual system: the eye, retina and visual pathways. [24 marks]

9 (a) Describe **one** study into the relationship between language and thought. [6 marks]
   (b) Outline and assess **one** explanation of the relationship between language and thought. [18 marks]

Section D – Developmental Psychology

10 (a) Describe one theory of cognitive development. [12 marks]
   (b) Evaluate this theory with reference to alternative explanations. [12 marks]

11 Discuss research into the formation of identity in adolescence. [24 marks]

12 Discuss research into cognitive changes in late adulthood. [24 marks]

A sample from a Psychology exam

In Unit 4 there are 12 marks for AO1 and 12 marks for AO2 in each question. (In Unit 5 there are 15 AO1 marks and 15 AO2.) These assessment objectives are the same as those used in your AS level exam. They are defined below.

Assessment objective 1 (AO1)

You should have **knowledge and understanding** of psychological theories, terminology, concepts, studies and methods in the core areas of cognitive, social, developmental, individual differences and physiological psychology, and communicate your knowledge and understanding of psychology in a clear and effective manner. At A2 you will be expected to extend your knowledge and understanding to psychological principles, perspectives and applications.

Assessment objective 2 (AO2)

You should **analyse and evaluate** psychological theories, concepts, studies and methods in the core areas of cognitive, social, developmental, individual differences and physiological psychology, and communicate your knowledge and understanding of psychology in a clear and effective manner. At A2 you will be expected to extend your analysis and evaluation to psychological principles, perspectives and applications.

Unlike the AS level exam, at A2 the AO1 questions are not always separated from the AO2 questions. They may be combined in various ways, as shown in the box below.

Examples of different AO1 and AO2 splits

Discuss **two** theories of visual perception. [24 marks]

'Discuss' is an **AO1** and **AO2** injunction which requires description (AO1) and evaluation (AO2) for 12 marks each.

(a) Outline **two** theories of visual perception. [12 marks]

(b) Evaluate these theories with reference to research evidence. [12 marks]

This question covers a similar topic area to the first essay title but in this case **AO1** has been separated from **AO2**. Part (a) is pure **AO1**, as indicated by the injunction '**outline**'. Part (b) is all **AO2**, as indicated by the injunction '**evaluate**'. In this case the form of evaluation is specified in the question.

(a) Describe **one** research study related to visual perception. [6 marks]

(b) Outline and evaluate **one** theory of visual perception. [18 marks]

In this question the **AO1** marks are split between part (a) and part (b), as indicated by the injunctions. In part (a) **description** of a study is required. Evaluation of this study would receive no credit. In part (b) one theory should be **outlined** (for a further 6 **AO1** marks) and should then be **evaluated** for the 12 **AO2** marks.

Each question contains an AO1 and an AO2 injunction. These injunctions tell you what to write.

For example, if the injunction is **'describe'** you must present your knowledge and understanding of the stipulated topic, because 'describe' is an AO1 injunction.

All the injunctions are shown in the box below.

AQA-A exam injunctions

AO1 terms

Describe, outline, explain, define	Require you to supply evidence of AO1.

Note that in addition:

Outline involves a summary description only (more breadth than detail/depth).

Define requires you to state what is meant by a particular term.

AO2 terms

Evaluate, assess, analyse, to what extent	Require you to supply evidence of AO2. Arguments should be informed and demonstrate an awareness of both strengths and limitations as far as possible.

AO1 and AO2 terms

Discuss, critically consider, compare and contrast	Require you both to describe (AO1) and evaluate (AO2) with reference to different if not contrasting points of view. This may be done sequentially or concurrently.

Note that in addition:

Compare and contrast requires you to demonstrate knowledge and understanding of the stipulated topic areas (AO1) and to evaluate/analyse similarities and/or differences between the stipulated topic areas (AO2).

Questions are set from the wording of the specification. The words used in the specification are combined with injunctions to form the questions so that you can feel confident about what sort of question you will have to answer. This means that you must **check the specification carefully** to ensure that you understand all the words and can satisfy all the requirements.

If a theory or study is given as an 'e.g.' in the specification, then no specific question can be set on this topic. The information is provided for guidance only. However, anything that is 'included' in the specification may be mentioned specifically in a question. For example, you could be asked to 'Discuss the nativist theory of language development' [because the specification states that you should study 'Explanations of language development, **including** environmental (**e.g.** learning) and nativist theories (e.g. Chomsky)']. However, you could not be asked to 'Discuss Chomsky's theory' because his name is only given as an 'e.g.'.

Some questions may be split into parts. There are occasions when questions are divided into two or even three parts. Over the whole question the AO1 and AO2 marks remain the same (12 and 12), but any one part may consist of a combination of these. The combinations are indicated by the injunctions that are used. Therefore, if part (a) of a question requires you to '*Describe* **one** theory of dreaming' (12 marks), then description only is required. If part (a) of a question requires you to '*Discuss* **one** theory of dreaming' (12 marks), then this breaks down to 6 marks for AO1 and 6 marks for AO2 because the injunction 'discuss' has been used (AO1 and AO2) and there are only 12 marks for this part of the question. Part (b) would then also have 6 marks for AO1 and 6 marks for AO2.

Be careful to note the particular requirements for each part of the question. If one part requires that you 'Evaluate theories in terms of their applications', you will only receive credit for this kind of evaluation and not for reference to alternate theories and/or research studies except insofar as they illuminate the value of the applications.

Quotations are used in some questions. The intention is to provide you with material that may inspire or challenge you to present a more searching response. In some cases the question following the quotation says '*With reference to the quotation*, discuss explanations of moral development'. In such cases **you must address the quotation in your response or you will lose some marks**. For high marks you must do more than just repeat the quotation; you must engage with it throughout the essay.

If there is a quotation but the subsequent question does not state 'with reference to the quotation', you need not address the quotation.

Numbers are specified where appropriate. Many questions require you to 'Discuss **one** theory' or 'Describe **two** studies' or 'Outline **two or more** explanations'. This is done in order to help you know what is sufficient for high marks. You must take heed of the number.

If only **one** theory is required, then **two** theories will not attract extra credit. They will both be marked and credit awarded for the best one. Describing two theories would have **wasted precious time** which would have been better spent on providing more detail of the first theory and/or using the second theory explicitly as a form of evaluation (if this is relevant to the question set).

If **two** theories are asked for then coverage of **one** theory will result in a penalty (called the **partial performance penalty**). This means that AO1 and AO2 are each marked out of a maximum of 8 marks.

If the phrase '**one or more**' is used, you may present more than one theory/study/explanation but one would be sufficient. **Numbers are there for your benefit.**

Examiners mark AQA–A exam questions using a standard set of descriptors. **After reading an essay the examiner must decide which band best describes the AO1 component of the essay and which band best describes the AO2 component of the essay.** The bands and descriptors are shown below.

After deciding on a band, the examiner then considers which *other* band was most tempting – the one just above the band selected or the one just below. This determines the actual mark given, e.g. whether 5 or 6 is selected.

For Unit 4 Assessment Objective 1 (AO1)

BAND	MARKS	CONTENT	RELEVANCE	ORGANISATION AND STRUCTURE	BREADTH AND DEPTH
3 (Top)	12–11	Accurate and well-detailed		Coherent	Substantial evidence of both and balance achieved
3 (Bottom)	10–9	Slightly limited, accurate and well-detailed		Coherent	Evidence of both but imbalanced
2 (Top)	8–7	Limited, accurate and reasonably detailed		Reasonably constructed	Increasing evidence of breadth and/or depth
2 (Bottom)	6–5	Limited, generally accurate but lacking in detail		Reasonably constructed	Some evidence of breadth and/or depth
1 (Top)	4–3	Basic, rudimentary, sometimes flawed	Sometimes focused		
1 (Bottom)	2–0	Just discernible; weak/muddled/inaccurate	Wholly/mainly irrelevant		

For Unit 4 Assessment Objective 2 (AO2)

BAND	MARKS	COMMENTARY	USE OF MATERIAL	SELECTION	ELABORATION
3 (Top)	12–11	Informed and thorough	Highly effective	Appropriate	Coherent
3 (Bottom)	10–9	Slightly limited	Effective	Appropriate	Coherent
2 (Top)	8–7	Reasonable but slightly limited	Effective		Evidence of coherent elaboration
2 (Bottom)	6–5	Reasonable but limited	Reasonably effective		Some evidence of elaboration
1 (Top)	4–3	Minimal, superficial and rudimentary	Restricted		
1 (Bottom)	2–0	Weak, muddled and incomplete	Wholly/mainly irrelevant		

Quality of written communication (QoWC)

In addition to AO1 and AO2, you will be awarded a mark on each unit paper for the quality of your written communication. Four marks are awarded on the basis of your ability to:
- **Select and use a form and style of writing appropriate to complex subject matter;**
- **Organise relevant information clearly and coherently, using specialist vocabulary;**
- **Present legible text and use accurate spelling, grammar and punctuation so that the meaning is clear.**

Synopticity and Unit 5

The Unit 5 paper is the most important examination of all. The mark for this paper is worth 20% of your final A level grade (AS is 50%, Unit 4 is 15% and coursework is 15%). Unit 5 is the exam that you must sit at the end of your studies. This paper aims to assess all of the knowledge you have accumulated over the whole course of psychology. This unit of the exam is assessed with reference to **synopticity**.

What is synopticity?

This is an assessment in all A level examinations that tests your understanding of the connections between the different elements of the subject, ensuring that you have an **overall grasp of the subject and not merely a number of separate modules of knowledge**.

An understanding of synopticity can be demonstrated by using the knowledge, understanding and skills learned in all your psychology studies. In particular this means:

- Knowledge and critical appreciation of **different approaches and perspectives** in psychology, such as the behavioural or cognitive approach.

- Knowledge and critical appreciation of **issues and debates** in psychology, such as ethics and reductionism.

- Appreciation of the **different methodologies** used in psychological investigations, such as experiments and observational studies.

- The ability to forge **links between topics** across the specification.

On Unit 5 you are assessed using the same marking criteria as for Unit 4, with the **addition of the synoptic criteria in both AO1 and AO2**. These additional criteria are:

- For AO1 you must aim to present **clear evidence of a range of different theoretical perspectives and/or methodological approaches relevant to the question.**

- For AO2 you must aim to present **clear critical commentary on the different theoretical perspectives and/or methodological approaches used in AO1.**

The questions on Unit 5 are **marked out of 30**, with an even split between AO1 and AO2 marks except for the **Approaches question**. The Approaches question is set in a completely different style to the others (see chapter 9) and has 12 AO1 marks and 18 AO2 marks.

The time allowed for Unit 5 is longer than for Unit 4. You have two hours to answer three questions. Therefore you have 40 minutes per question.

The higher marks for each question and longer time for answering reflect the importance of this unit paper. Chapters 6, 7 and 8 in this book contain 'synoptic signposts' which give you extra help on how to plan your answers to synoptic questions.

1 Social Psychology

Exam Questions

Time allowed: 30 minutes

Question 1

Outline and evaluate **two** theories of the origins of prejudice. [24 marks]

Question 2

'There are many types of relationships that psychology has yet to fully explore. Indeed we might justifiably argue that our understanding of human relationships is limited to a narrow range of possible types, and that we know very little about variations on this theme.'

Discuss what psychologists have discovered about 'understudied relationships' (e.g. gay and lesbian, and Internet relationships). [24 marks]

Question 3

(a) Outline **two** explanations of human altruism. [12 marks]
(b) Assess the extent to which there are cultural differences in such behaviour. [12 marks]

How to 'deconstruct' a question and plan an effective answer

This section deals with Question 1 above.

Mark allocation

- This question requires you to demonstrate two skills, **AO1** (knowledge and understanding) and **AO2** (analysis and evaluation). These are indicated by the 'injunctions' used in the question. '**Outline**' is the AO1 term and '**evaluate**' is the AO2 term. Half the available marks are for the AO1 content of the answer, and half for the AO2 content. **Answers that fail to address both of these skills,** or provide them in a very unbalanced way, will **lose the opportunity to pick up the marks available for that component**. No matter how good the AO1 content, the maximum mark is still only 12 if no AO2 evaluation is present. It is important to understand exactly the requirements of this question. It asks for **two** theories (not one or more than two), so presenting a general response that does not focus on two theories in particular misses the point of the question. It is also important that **you** are clear in **your** mind which two theories you have chosen for this question. It might well be useful (for you **and** the examiner) to identify these at the start of your essay.

Planning your response

- **Prejudice** can be defined as 'a **learned attitude toward a target object, involving negative affect**' (Zimbardo et al. 1995). Note that this definition is included here simply to place what follows in context. There is no requirement, given the wording of the question, for you to offer such a definition in your answer. It **does**, however, help you to get it clear in your mind exactly what you are trying to explain in the paragraphs that follow.

● There are 30 minutes allowed for this question, so we can divide the answer into four convenient 7.5-minute 'chunks' (each one about 150 words) to aid the precision of our response. There is a temptation, with questions like this, to include a lot of irrelevant information that the question simply doesn't require. Definition, explanations of the different components of a prejudicial attitude, attempts at prejudice reduction etc. are **not** required, and would not earn marks. An effective structure would be:

1 An **outline** (i.e. a **summary description**) of the first theory of the origins of prejudice.
2 An **evaluation** of the first theory of the origins of prejudice.
3 An **outline** of the second theory of the origins of prejudice.
4 An **evaluation** of the second theory of the origins of prejudice.

⊚ Paragraph 1

● Since you do not need to define or otherwise introduce the topic of prejudice, **you should start trying to earn as many marks as you can as early as you can**. Having established what your first theory might be (appropriate theories would include the authoritarian personality theory, realistic conflict theory, social identity theory and so on), you should offer an outline description of this theory in your first paragraph. This should be a précis of your chosen theory (this takes practice) in about 150 words. If you choose **realistic conflict theory** as your first theory, the paragraph might contain the following:

■ If members of one group believe that their interests can only be satisfied at the expense of some other group, then hostility develops between the groups concerned. When groups are engaged in competitive activities, each group will develop negative attitudes towards the other group (the **out-group**).
■ The theory was first formulated by Sherif (1966). During the **Robbers' Cave** study (1953), Sherif noticed how boys could be induced to display openly hostile behaviour towards other groups of boys, simply as a result of introducing competition between them.
■ As a result of this experiment, Sherif concluded that **intergroup bias and hostility** develops through **competition** and can be reduced through co-operation in pursuit of superordinate goals.
■ Brewer and Campbell (1976) carried out a study of 30 tribal groups in East Africa. Consistent with realistic conflict theory, groups in close proximity with each other were be more likely to be involved in disputes over access to scarce resources.

⊚ Paragraph 2

● There are many effective ways of providing an 'evaluation' of your theories of the origins of prejudice. These include assessing the **implications** of a theory, assessing the **extent of research support** or looking at **inconsistencies** in the theory itself. Remember that the highest marks are for **effective evaluation**, so don't just list points that may be appropriate. Say **why** your point of evaluation detracts from (or even enhances) the value of the theory being evaluated. Appropriate evaluative content might include:

■ **Realistic conflict theory** has a number of advantages over other explanations of prejudice. Particularly important in this respect is its **ability to explain the 'ebb and flow' of prejudice over time or different social contexts** (e.g. in Nazi Germany or the former Yugoslavia).
■ Whilst it is not difficult to understand the resilience of in-group bias when groups are engaged in competition for some scarce resource, it is harder to explain when **no such competition exists yet prejudice clearly does.**

- A related problem concerns the fact that **competition does not even appear to be necessary** for in-group favouritism to develop. It appears that people will favour their group over another merely as a result of being **categorised** in that group rather than another (Tajfel et al. 1971).

Paragraph 3

- If you are following the outline, evaluate, outline, evaluate route through this essay, you should now be halfway through and ready to begin your outline description of the second theory. The question allows for any appropriate theory of the origins of prejudice, and **social identity theory** follows on nicely from the last point of the second paragraph.

    - Tajfel (1982) believed that the mere **categorisation** of people into groups was **sufficient for prejudice to develop between the groups**. Contrary to the claims of realistic conflict theory, the fact that two distinct groups exist seems sufficient for the creation of group identities which then take precedence over group members' individual identities.
    - Social identity theory suggests that we use this categorisation in order to **enhance our self-esteem**. Our social identity consists of how we define ourselves in each of our social categories. As people strive for a **positive** social identity, this is derived from favourable social comparisons made between the in-group and other social groups.
    - When we compare ourselves with others, we highlight qualities that support our own in-group values (termed '**in-group favouritism**') and we point out any weaknesses that may appear to exist in the out-group (termed '**negative out-group bias**').

Paragraph 4

- **Time management is vital** in an essay like this. It is easy to get carried away and write far more than you should in the preceding three paragraphs. Just think, an extra minute in each of the preceding paragraphs leaves **fewer than 5 minutes** for this final evaluative paragraph. However, if you have been careful with your time, you will have enough for a telling evaluation of the second theory. Remember that **research support** is a good way of evaluating the worth of a particular theory. Appropriate content might include:

    - A problem with realistic conflict theory is that prejudice was still evident **without** realistic competition between groups. Social identity theory is able to explain this through the concept of **social competition**, which reflects the need that people have for a positive self-image, even at the expense of others.
    - A number of studies have supported the assumption that group membership has implications for an individual's social identity (e.g. Cialdini et al.'s 1976 study of **football supporters**).
    - There is a great deal of evidence that people will engage in intergroup comparisons of the sort predicted by the theory **when asked to do so**, but few studies have found evidence of **spontaneous** comparisons.

EMILE'S ANSWER TO QUESTION 2

'There are many types of relationships that psychology has yet to fully explore. Indeed we might justifiably argue that our understanding of human relationships is limited to a narrow range of possible types, and that we know very little about variations on this theme.'

Discuss what psychologists have discovered about 'understudied relationships' (e.g. gay and lesbian, and Internet relationships). [24 marks]

> Although helpful to the reader, there is no need to offer a 'menu' of what is to come. You will *not receive credit* for your *intention* to cover a point, whereas you *will* receive credit for your later discussion of the material. Emile has included a definition of 'understudied relationships' that provides a *good context* for any discussion that follows. This is a *direct response* to the question, in that Emile suggests that, prior to 1995, psychologists knew very little about this area.

In this essay I am going to discuss two different types of 'understudied' relationship, gay and lesbian relationships, and Internet relationships. I will look at research evidence for these different types of relationships, and show how they may differ from the more usual heterosexual and non-Internet relationships. Understudied relationships, as defined by Duck (1995), are all those variations on Western, heterosexual and interpersonal relationships that psychology has not tended to study. Most, if not all of the social psychological research on relationships up that point had, as suggested in the quotation, ignored any variations on this theme.

Kitzinger (2001) suggests a number of ways that gay and lesbian relationships differ from heterosexual relationships. One of these is that in heterosexual relationships, gender differences often account for the different roles that each person plays in the relationship (e.g. who cooks and cleans, and who goes out to work). In same-sex relationships this is not the case as the partners cannot turn to traditional gender differences to guide them. Kitzinger claims that this leaves gay and lesbian partners free to make their own choices about who takes responsibility for what and that this is largely a matter of negotiation between them.

> This is a *very good summary* of one of Kitzinger's main arguments about the differences between heterosexual and homosexual relationships. The first part of Emile's assertion (i.e. showing the difference between heterosexual and homosexual relationships in this regard) would count as *AO1* description, and the latter part (i.e. the implication of this difference) as *AO2* commentary. It is a good idea to *think critically* about your descriptive material, constantly asking yourself the simple question 'so what?'

Not all homosexual relationships are the same, however. Kitzinger suggests that lesbian relationships are influenced by the socialisation experiences that the two women have had during their development as women. Particularly in the Western world, women have still internalised what it means to be 'a woman'. This then influences how they are in their relationship with another woman. For example, women tend to be socialised into the 'caring and sharing' role, and men into more emotionally distant roles. As a result of these differences between men and women in our culture, lesbian relationships tend to be characterised by more emotional closeness and gay relationships by more emotional distance. Kitzinger suggested that one consequence of these differences was that gay men were more likely to have affairs than were lesbians.

An added problem of being gay or lesbian is that when people do 'come out', they often find their sexual identities denied by their parents, who might suggest that they will 'grow out of it'. A consequence of this is that lack of parental acknowledgement and support can lead to self-doubt in their gay and lesbian children. This also means that gay and lesbian teenagers are denied the opportunity to explore possible homosexual relationships in the way that heterosexual teenagers would do. Homosexual couples also experience considerable prejudice from those around them and this has led to discrimination against gay and lesbian couples being seen as an infringement of human rights. However, even though this is the case, it does not make it any easier for homosexual couples to build and maintain their relationships within a society that is so obviously hostile towards them.

Although accurate, Emile doesn't really tell us much that is *specific* to on-line relationships. He suggests that 'many of the normal features of attraction' are missing from on-line relationships, but neglects to mention what these might be. The 'rules of self-disclosure' apply equally to on-line and face-to-face relationships, therefore the material being used as AO1 content is only *marginally effective* in this context. It would have been much better to have indicated areas where on-line relationships *differed* from face-to-face relationships. Unlike the previous paragraphs, there is nothing in this paragraph that might count as AO2 content.

On-line relationships are another type of understudied relationship. Lea and Spears (1995) claim that psychologists have tended to restrict their interest to relationships that are 'conducted in the open'. Using the Internet becomes a new way for people to find each other, although many of the normal features of attraction do not happen in an on-line relationship. At the beginning of a 'relationship' a person may be interacting with a complete stranger (i.e. someone they have never met in real life). The rules of self-disclosure mean that they are discouraged from expressing any personal feelings. As the relationship develops, this means they begin to disclose more and more. Lea and Spears also found that heavy users of e-mail are more likely to use the computer to 'make new friends and initiate relationships' whereas 'light' users tend to build relationships in other ways.

15/24

How to score full marks

Know where you are going but don't tell the examiner

- We are told from an early age that there are 'rules' for writing good essays. These 'rules' include telling the reader what you are going to write about and then summarising your arguments at the end. This is admirable advice but not appropriate in the strict time confines of a 30-minute examination essay. **Instead of wasting time and words telling the examiner what you are going to do** (you will get **no credit** for this), just **go ahead and do it**. It is, of course, vital that you know what you are going to do, and have any plan clearly worked out in your mind or on paper, but the examiner should, hopefully, be able to work it out for him or herself.

Keep an eye on the commentary

- It is an inescapable fact that there are as many AO2 marks for each question as there are AO1 marks. Emile doesn't always appear aware of this equity within questions and tends to spend more time **describing** than he does **evaluating**. He is, however, quite astute in using fairly simple strategies to create AO2 commentary in the earlier paragraphs. Sometimes students use the tactic of sticking down the words 'however' and 'but' every so often in an attempt to convince the examiner they are doing something more than describing when they are not. Emile's technique is more subtle and convincing than that. He constantly **engages with the descriptive material to draw out its implications and consequences**. There is an important lesson here – **evaluation** (judging the value of something) is more than just 'slagging it off'; it can include **judging its worth through an examination of its implications** (what if this were true?) and **consequences** (what might this lead to?). Unfortunately, this technique lets Emile down in the final paragraph as he neglected to do anything worthwhile to pick up AO2 marks.

Keep it informed

- Questions on relationships often tend to evoke masses of anecdotal material or snippets of information picked up from magazines, the television or even from conversations down at the pub. The purpose of a psychology examination is to assess the **psychology** you have acquired during your study of the subject. As you can see from Emile's answer, what is required is not vastly complicated, but rather an **informed**, **psychological** and **thoughtfully critical response** to a pretty straightforward and predictable question set from the AQA specification. Moral? **Know your specification, and be prepared to air your psychological knowledge of it when called upon to do so**.

Question to try

Question 3

(a) Outline **two** explanations of human altruism. [12 marks]

(b) Assess the extent to which there are cultural differences in such behaviour.
[12 marks]

[Time allowed: 30 minutes]

Examiner's hints

● It is well worth investing a little time to think through this question **carefully**. It is in two distinct parts. The first asks for an outline of **two** explanations of human altruism, and the second an assessment of the extent to which there are **cultural differences** in such behaviour. When choosing whether to answer a question such as this, ask yourself whether you can do **both** parts of the question justice, or whether you should look elsewhere.

● Although the question asks for explanations of **altruistic** behaviour, explanations of other forms of helping behaviour (that may have more selfish motivations but **appear** altruistic) would be just as appropriate. So, Cialdini's **negative-state relief model** is just as appropriate as Batson's **empathy-altruism model**.

● In the first part of the question, you are asked to **outline** your two explanations. This effectively calls for a **précis** of these two explanations, which is quite a difficult thing to do, especially where there is such a time pressure on you (two explanations in 15 minutes). It is worth **preparing** for questions such as this by **practising** writing approximately 150-word summaries that give the gist of a particular explanation without getting bogged down in unnecessary detail.

● Sometimes, as here, questions have quite **specific** requirements for the AO2 part of your answer (in this question it is an assessment of **cultural differences** in altruistic behaviour). It is not appropriate in response to part (b) of this question to simply offer an evaluation of the two explanations from part (a). Nor would it be appropriate to include this evaluation in part (a) because this only requires AO1 material. So ask yourself, 'What do I know about that?' **before** selecting this question.

● Remember, the second part of the question is the part that assesses your **AO2** skills. What you include here, therefore, should be more than a straightforward **description** of cultural differences in altruistic behaviour, but an assessment of the **extent** of such differences. Therefore you might present evidence that **supports** or **challenges** the belief that there are cultural differences, examine the **impact** of such differences, or perhaps offer an **interpretation** of these differences (for example, in terms of the individualist/collectivist identity of cultures).

2 Physiological Psychology

Time allowed: 30 minutes

Question 1

(a) Outline **one** invasive and **one** non-invasive method used to investigate the brain.

[12 marks]

(b) Assess the strengths and limitations of each of the methods for investigating the brain that you outlined in part (a). [12 marks]

Question 2

Describe and evaluate **one** theory of the functions of dreaming. [24 marks]

Question 3

Discuss research relating to the role of brain structures in emotional behaviour and experience. [24 marks]

How to 'deconstruct' a question and plan an effective answer

This section deals with Question 1 above.

Mark allocation

● This question is split into two parts, with the first part being all **AO1** (knowledge and understanding) and the second **AO2** (analysis and evaluation). This is not always the case, as some divided questions contain both AO1 and AO2 in both parts. It pays, therefore, to know what each of the examination 'injunctions' means in terms of its AO1 or AO2 requirement. In this question, **'outline'** is the AO1 term in part (a) and **'assess'** is the AO2 term in part (b). Note that the second part of the question asks you to assess **strengths and limitations**, so don't just cover the positive or negative points of your chosen methods. It is also important to understand exactly what is meant by the terms **invasive** and **non-invasive** in this context. These are referred to explicitly in the AQA specification, so make sure you choose one of each, rather than two invasive (or two non-invasive), and identify which is which.

Planning your response

● In this context 'invasive' refers to any procedure that 'invades' the body in some way. There is a fine line between what might be considered invasive and what non-invasive, and indeed there is a case for procedures such as the PET scan (used here as an example of a non-invasive procedure) to be seen as invasive. However, procedures such as surgical interventions (electrical stimulation, lesions etc.) and those involving drugs are generally seen as **invasive**, whereas scanning and imaging procedures (CT, MRI, PET etc.) are seen as **non-invasive**.

- You should approach this question very carefully, as your **time management skills** will be tested to their limit. There are 30 minutes allowed for this question, so we can divide the answer into four convenient 7.5-minute 'chunks' (each one about 150 words) to aid the precision of our response. Remember, you are required to assess **both strengths and limitations of each method**, so that must be taken into consideration when planning your response. Your answer might be structured as follows.

  1 An **outline** (i.e. a summary description) of your **invasive** method for studying the brain.
  2 An **outline** of your **non-invasive** method for studying the brain.
  3 An **assessment** of the strengths and limitations of your invasive method.
  4 An **assessment** of the strengths and limitations of your non-invasive method.

🎯 Paragraph 1

- You might begin this paragraph explaining what electrical stimulation of the brain (ESB) is all about.

  - ESB involves the application of a **weak electrical current** to a specific area of the brain. By adjusting the current, a **'false' nerve impulse** is produced which 'fools' the brain into thinking that it has received an impulse from one of its sensory receptors.
  - A computer is used to analyse the responses produced by a series of stimuli. This process can thus be used to **identify areas of the brain involved in different sensory processes**.
- You should then, logically, describe the **effects** of ESB and why these are useful to researchers.

  - Electrical stimulation of a particular brain structure usually has behavioural effects that are the **opposite** of those produced when the same area is lesioned.
  - Early studies using this technique enabled physiologists to draw a 'map' of the human cortex, relating specific areas of the **cortex** to specific **muscle activity**.

🎯 Paragraph 2

- In many questions there is opportunity for you to address each of the skills (AO1 and AO2) in any order you like, but in this question the AO1 material makes up part (a) of your response. Don't be tempted to split your answer in a different way to that required by the question. This second paragraph will thus be a description of your non-invasive method. As before, you might begin with a description of what a PET scan actually is and the information it provides:

  - **Positron emission tomography** (**PET**) scans provide information about the **metabolic activity** of the brain.
  - First, the patient receives an injection of **radioactive 2-deoxyglucose** (2-DG) which, because of its similarity to glucose, is taken up rapidly by the neurons in the brain. Unlike glucose, 2-DG cannot be metabolised and therefore accumulates in the active neurons until it is broken down and released.
  - As the radioactive molecules of 2-DG decay, they emit subatomic particles called **positrons**, which are detected by the PET scanner.
  - A computer then determines which areas of the brain have taken up the radioactive substance, and it produces a picture of a slice of the brain, showing the **activity level** of various regions within that slice.

🎯 Paragraph 3

- If you are following the 4 × 150-word paragraphs rule, the second half of your essay, and the last two paragraphs, should be assessing the strengths and limitations of your two chosen methods. There is no requirement that you divide each paragraph equally into material relevant to strengths and material relevant to limitations, but you should try to have a **reasonable balance**.

- Appropriate material with which to assess the **strengths** of ESB procedures include:
  - ESB has provided us with **invaluable information** about how the brain works and, it is claimed, has also been valuable in **treating** a variety of different conditions.
  - Electrical stimulation has been shown to have useful applications in the **reduction of pain**, where stimulation of particular locations within the brain can cause analgesia. The same technique has been used in reducing chronic pain in humans.
  - ESB has enabled investigators to reach important conclusions about the **connections** between various parts of the brain and the **involvement** of any one area of the brain in particular behaviours.

- Appropriate material with which to assess the **limitations** of ESB procedures include:
  - The effects of ESB may be **different** at different times, with subjects tending to experience different emotions or produce different behaviours in response to the same stimulation at different times.
  - Behaviour produced as a result of ESB does **not** perfectly mimic natural behaviour, being more **compulsive** and **stereotypical**.
  - Valenstein (1977) claims that no single area of the brain is likely to be the sole source of a behaviour or emotion. He suggests that the belief that the brain is organised into neat compartments that can be discovered by ESB is simply a **myth**.

◎ Paragraph 4

- If you have managed to keep to your timing, you should be now ready to embark on the final paragraph which, for the purposes of this illustration, is an assessment of the strengths and limitations of PET scans for studying the brain.

- Appropriate material with which to assess the **strengths** of PET scans include:
  - PET scans have been useful in **diagnosing abnormalities** in the brain (such as tumours), and can give surgeons vital information prior to surgery.
  - PET scans have also been used to investigate **possible differences** in the brain activity of people with and without a particular psychological disorder, e.g. the pattern of neural activity in the brains of schizophrenics has been discovered to be different to that of non-schizophrenics.
  - The ability to **correlate activity in different brain areas with psychological functioning** has made PET, and newer versions such as SPET (single photon emission tomography), scans the most useful of current computer-based techniques.

- Appropriate material with which to assess the **limitations** of PET scans include:
  - With current versions of the PET scan there are problems of **spatial** resolution (how small an area of tissue can be studied) and **temporal** resolution (the frequency of brain activity that can be studied – the brain typically acts in milliseconds). Newer variations such as SPET have largely overcome such problems.
  - These techniques are extremely **expensive** and **time-consuming**, and machines that can carry out such procedures are found only in the largest research hospitals.

JAMIE'S ANSWER TO QUESTION 2

Describe and evaluate **one** theory of the functions of dreaming. [24 marks]

Freud referred to dreams as the 'royal road to the unconscious', and gave them special significance as an arena in which wish fulfilment could take place without the normal sanctions that we experience in our waking state. If the content of the dream was disturbing or frightening, it would intrude into consciousness and wake the dreamer up. Therefore the content of a dream must be disguised so this does not take place. Thoughts and objects are transformed in the dream into symbols, many of which are seen as having a sexual meaning. According to Freud, no matter how absurd the content of a dream appears, it has meaning for the dreamer. The exact meaning of a dream could be determined by analysing it in the context of the person's waking life and so give a clue to that person's fears and wishes.

Freud's theory of dreams claims that dreams are a safety valve which let people harmlessly deal with wishes and urges in their unconscious mind that would be considered unacceptable when they are awake. When people are awake, these impulses are kept out of the conscious mind because of their unacceptable nature. In our dreams, however, the expression of these impulses gratifies our unconscious desires. Freud said that our unconscious desires are not gratified directly in dreams. He claimed that the manifest content of the dream (the dream as reported by the dreamer) is a censored and symbolic version of the latent content (its real meaning). Freud believed that the meaning of a dream must be 'disguised' because it consisted of wishes and desires that would be disturbing if expressed directly. As a result of this the dream contains a sort of symbolic representation of our real desires.

Freud therefore believed that dreams provided a valuable insight into the motives that guided a person's behaviour. He believed that dreams often revealed deeply hidden conflicts, although because of their disguised nature it was difficult to find out what these conflicts actually were. In therapy, the therapist had to interpret the manifest content of a dream to get at the underlying latent content. Some of Freud's patients reported dreams where a loved one (often the father) was harmed in some way. Freud believed that such dreams represented unconscious anger or resentment towards the father, feelings that originated from the Oedipus

---

This is a decent first paragraph, although some of this material is more concerned with the *nature* of dreams within Freudian theory than the *function* of dreams. With just a little work on the part of the reader, though, it is possible to extract from this the primary function of dream sleep according to this theory.

Another paragraph very much along the lines of the first. Indeed it *repeats* some of the points made in the first paragraph so would get *no extra credit* for them here. Be careful not to repeat yourself in answers as *material cannot be double credited.*

A good paragraph, *clear, accurate* and *not repeating* previous material. It also *explicitly addresses* the 'functions' of dreams as asked for in the question. Worryingly though, this is the third paragraph, and all the material so far has been AO1. By now, Jamie should have presented some AO2 evaluation.

At last some AO2. There is really only one point here, although it is handled very well, and is used *effectively*. The inclusion of Hobson and McCarley's activation-synthesis theory is *not integrated into the answer* in an effective way. It is woefully insufficient to try to link other explanations with the phrase 'There are other theories that explain dreams in a different way.' To be effectively used it could be *contrasted* with Freud's theory in some way so as to point out deficiencies in the Freudian perspective on dreams.

complex, the young boy's jealousy about his father's sexual relationship with his mother. Psychoanalysts believe that the dream disguises these wishes in order to protect the dreamer from the discomfort of knowing that he or she wishes harm towards a parent.

Critics of Freud's interpretation of dreams claim that many of his explanations appeared far-fetched, and that there was no objective way in which an analyst's interpretation of a dream could be checked against reality. McIlveen and Gross (1996) suggest that the interpretation of a dream is not something that can be objectively achieved even if the interpreter is a trained psychoanalyst. Even Freud appeared to agree with this because he said that not everything in a dream is symbolic, and sometimes 'a cigar is just a cigar'. There are other theories that explain dreams in a different way. For example, the 'activation synthesis theory' of dreaming (Hobson & McCarley 1977) sees dreams as essentially random and meaningless.

14/24

How to score full marks

Select your theory carefully

● There is a danger when answering an examination question such as this to try to slip in a prepared answer on sleep, e.g. the function of dreaming is to sleep. Many students try this, and inevitably lose most if not all of the marks available. There are lots of theories that deal explicitly with dreams and these are being questioned here. When choosing your theory, you should choose the one that you feel you could answer in the most **balanced** way. In other words, some theories lend themselves more to critical evaluation than do others. This is particularly the case with theories that have been subjected to empirical investigation. Freud's theory of dreams has universal appeal among students, for whatever reason, but does not lend itself to easy evaluation. Perhaps Jamie might have been better off choosing an alternative theory which **did** lend itself more to effective evaluation, and therefore given himself more opportunity to access decent marks for **both** skills.

⊙ Do a little research

● With some theories, there is a fairly simple idea that is easily grasped and then you may be left with very little else to write about. In such situations there is a temptation to repeat what you have already said in a slightly different way. Jamie has revisited at least two of the points from the first paragraph in paragraph two. There is a simple lesson here. **Learn what is required in the different areas of the specification** and then **prepare** your response in advance. Don't rely just on your notes or your course textbook. Read around, use the Internet and **find out** as much as you can about the theories you have chosen to study. Jamie seemed to be taken by surprise that he might have to evaluate Freud's theory of dreams and was totally unprepared for this eventuality. With some advance planning, and **focused** revision, he could have balanced his answer so much more effectively.

⊙ Keep an eye on the mark allocations

● In the introduction to this book, we gave you an indication of how marks are allocated for each question. It is wise to keep this in mind as you compose your response to this question. If Jamie had done that, he might have remembered that the difference between 4 and 8 marks for AO2 is not that great, and therefore he might have turned what is a decent answer into a very good one **without too much extra material**. Overall, an answer like this would receive about 10 marks for AO1 and about 4 marks for AO2, giving **14 marks overall**, which is equivalent to a **Grade C**.

Question to try

Question 3

Discuss research relating to the role of brain structures in emotional behaviour and experience. [24 marks]

[Time allowed: 30 minutes]

Examiner's hints

- The AQA definition of the word 'research' allows for both **theoretical** and **empirical** insights (in that both are part of the research 'cycle'). Either or both of these approaches would be appropriate here. Some students might concentrate on models of emotion, others on research studies of emotion, and others on an integration of the two.

- It is important to note that the question asks for the role of **brain structures** in emotional behaviour and experience, therefore you should be careful about using **theories** of emotional experience without using these within this context. The **James-Lange** theory and the **Cannon-Bard** theory both could be relevant here, but you should think carefully about what they have to say about brain structures rather than simply describing and evaluating the theories as a whole.

- The AQA specification is quite specific about this topic area. The exact wording of the specification is 'The role of brain structures (e.g. hypothalamus, limbic system, cerebral cortex) in emotional behaviour and experience', so a question on this topic should not come as a surprise in the examination. It **is** a complex area, but that should not prevent you from **reading around the area in advance** so that you are more fully engaged with it as an examination topic. By doing your own reading, using secondary sources or even the Internet, you are making your material more **interesting** and therefore more **memorable**.

- This question has what is technically known as a **plurality requirement**. This simply means you need to write about more than one brain structure (note that the question says brain **structures** in the plural). The specification gives a number of structures as examples (hypothalamus, limbic system, cerebral cortex), although these are only examples rather than prescribed areas that you must address.

3 Cognitive Psychology

Exam Questions

Time allowed: 30 minutes

Question 1

Describe and evaluate **two or more** explanations of divided attention.   [24 marks]

Question 2

Discuss the structure and functions of the visual system: the eye, retina and visual pathways.   [24 marks]

Question 3

(a) Describe **one** study into the relationship between language and thought.

[6 marks]

(b) Outline and assess **one** explanation of the relationship between language and thought.

[18 marks]

How to 'deconstruct' a question and plan an effective answer

This section deals with Question 3 above.

Mark allocation

● This question is in two parts and the marks appear to be unevenly split. However, there are still 12 marks for **AO1** (knowledge and understanding) and 12 marks for **AO2** (analysis and evaluation), as in all AQA-A A2 level questions. In this question the **AO1** marks have been divided between part (a) and part (b).

● In part (a) you are required to describe a study for 6 marks. This is **half** of the available **AO1** marks. In part (b) you must outline **one** explanation of the relationship between language and thought. 'Outline' is an **AO1** injunction requiring a **description of the topic in summary form**, i.e. focusing on breadth rather than depth (detail). There are 6 **AO1** marks available for this outline.

● The remaining marks for part (b) are for your assessment (evaluation) of this explanation. 'Assess' is an **AO2** injunction requiring you to **make an informed judgement about how good or effective the explanation is**.

● The question asks you to describe **one** study and outline **one** explanation. If you include more than one study, both will be read by the examiner and marks awarded to the best description. The same applies to the explanation.

⌖Planning your response

● In part (a) you should select a suitable study for description, and then a suitable explanation for part (b). This is likely to be the linguistic relativity hypothesis since this explanation is included in the specification. You can assess this explanation in numerous ways, most obviously through a **consideration of other research studies that both support and challenge the hypothesis**. You can extend your assessment by offering **contrasting explanations**, as long as you do this **effectively** as part of a **sustained critical commentary** rather than simply describing further explanations.

● **It is vital that you match the time spent on the parts of this question to the available marks.** If you spend half the allocated time in describing a study but only a few minutes outlining your explanation, **you will limit your overall mark** because you cannot be given more than 6 marks for the study. You should spend approximately 7 minutes on part (a), 7 minutes on outlining the explanation, and a final 14 minutes assessing this explanation. This would result in the following plan of four 'chunks', each of about 150 words:

1 A **description** of one study (part (a)).
2 An **outline** (i.e. summary description) of one explanation.
3 An **assessment** of the explanation by **considering research studies.**
4 An **assessment** of the explanation by **considering alternative explanations and/or flaws in the explanation's logic.**

⌖Paragraph 1

● When describing a study it may be helpful to use the guidelines from your AS studies, i.e. cover **aims, procedures, findings and conclusions** where you know such details. This would ensure **depth as well as breadth**. An obvious study to use would be one of those by Loftus that demonstrated how language affects memory.

■ Loftus and Palmer (1974) aimed to find out to what extent recall is affected by the actual words used to describe a car accident. They showed a film of a car accident and asked participants to estimate the speed the cars were going when they hit each other.
■ If the word 'smashed' was used instead of 'hit' participants estimated higher speeds. This shows that the **perception was influenced by the language** (leading questions) used.
■ In a follow-up study, participants returned to the laboratory after a week and were asked to recall aspects of the car accident, most importantly 'Did you see any broken glass?'. The group given the word 'smashed' in the original descriptions were twice as likely to answer 'yes' to seeing broken glass (though there was none) than those who had the word 'hit'. This shows the **effects of postevent information on later recall**.

⌖Paragraph 2

● The beginning of part (b) must **focus on one explanation** of the relationship between language and thought. In order to write sufficient material to earn 6 marks, **you may need to use examples** that address the requirement to **provide an explanation** of this relationship. **Do not waste time providing unnecessary background details.**

■ Whorf (1956) first outlined the linguistic relativity hypothesis, arguing that we 'dissect nature along the lines laid down by our native languages'. Many of our experiences are **ambiguous** and the language we speak provides us with a way of **resolving ambiguities and categorising experience**. This affects the way we think.
■ The language spoken in one country differs from languages used in other countries, and **these differences can be related to different ways of thinking**. For example, if a person's native language has no past tense this shapes the world view of the speakers.

- Such linguistic relativity **affects the development of thinking in children** because the words that are used in their native language shape their thought. Linguistic relativity also affects adult thinking when they learn about new things.
- The classic example used to illustrate this is of **Eskimos and snow**. Whorf claimed that the Eskimos had lots of words for snow and this **vocabulary enabled them to make finer distinctions**. The same can be said for any group of people with unique experiences.

Paragraph 3

- The remaining parts of the essay are concerned with **evaluation**. There are no hard and fast rules about how to do this. However, it is important that you **demonstrate the extent to which your evaluation is informed by psychological research and is thorough**, i.e. you should consider more than one form of evaluation. You also must provide **coherent elaboration**, i.e. state the criticisms and explain (elaborate) it in the context of the essay.

  - Miller and McNeill (1969) suggest that there are **three versions** of Whorf's hypothesis. The 'strong' claim is that **thought is determined by language**; a 'weaker' hypothesis is that **language affects perception**; and the weakest hypothesis is that **language affects memory**. Perception and memory are forms of thinking.
  - The fact that deaf people with little language are capable of thought (Furth 1966) **challenges** the strong hypothesis. Carroll and Casagrande (1958) claimed that Navaho children demonstrated different ways of thinking if they only spoke Navaho rather than Navaho and English. However, being bilingual might have slowed their progress.
  - Heider (1972) showed that the Dani in New Guinea had better recall for focal colours (colours that appear to be related to our perceptual system such as fire-engine red), despite having only two basic colour words. This suggests that **perception is independent of language**. However, Schooler and Engstler-Schooler (1990) found that participants who had to label colours were less accurate on a colour recognition task, suggesting that **colour memory was distorted by language** in the form of labelling.
  - The study by Loftus showed that language can affect memory. There is other **support** for this, such as Carmichael et al. (1932), who found that recall of shapes was related to the labels provided during initial exposure.

Paragraph 4

- In the final paragraph you should move towards a conclusion, **weighing up the research evidence and considering alternative explanations.**

  - The research evidence tends to support the view that language affects memory and is likely to affect perception but that it does not determine thought. There are some challenges to this conclusion. For example, Sinclair-de-Zwart (1969) found that children who could not conserve had differences in their vocabularies, but also that simply teaching them the vocabulary did not lead to cognitive development.
  - Whorf's example of the Eskimos has been challenged by Pinker (1994), who argues that the Eskimos actually only have around 12 words for snow, and we have a similar number in English. Even if Eskimos did have more words, it wouldn't be surprising.
  - Hunt and Agnoli (1991) have suggested a **modified** version of Whorf's hypothesis, the view that **different languages make it easier to express certain concepts** and this would make it easier to think in that way.

If you know the details of the visual system this question may seem like a gift, but there is a danger, as in Jack's case, that you devote *too much time to providing details* and leave *insufficient time for the AO2 material*. It is vital that you are able to accurately *summarise your knowledge*. There is *some credit in the first paragraph* towards AO2 through the comment given on the *effect of the blind spot on perception. Time was wasted* in this first paragraph by including details of a little activity to illustrate the blind spot. Such activities may increase your understanding of key concepts but are *not creditworthy in an exam*.

JACK'S ANSWER TO QUESTION 2

Discuss the structure and functions of the visual system: the eye, retina and visual pathways. [24 marks]

The visual system consists of the eye, retina and visual pathways. Light is received in the eye and recorded at the retina by photosensitive cells. The eye consists of the pupil for letting in light and the lens for focusing the light on the back of the eye. It is filled with vitreous humour to maintain its shape and movement is controlled by muscles. There are two types of photosensitive cells. One type (rods) respond to shades of grey, to movement and to edges. They function in conditions of low lighting and are concentrated in the outer parts of the retina. Other photosensitive cells (cones) are sensitive to colour and function in daylight conditions. Photoreceptors are connected to bipolar cells as well as amacrine and horizontal cells. Bipolar cells are connected to ganglion cells in the third layer which is actually closer to the source of light. From the ganglion cells nerves pass across the retina and are bundled together as one fibre that leaves the eye through the optic disc (blind spot). You might think that this would disrupt vision but there are all sorts of imperfections in the retinal image and the brain fills in the gaps so that you can only be aware of the blind spot if you specially look for it (e.g. by looking at a dot on a piece of paper with one eye while the other is covered, a second dot that is 6 inches away should disappear as you move the paper towards you).

From the eye nervous impulses are passed to the visual cortex but they crossover at the optic chiasma. Information from the left visual field of both eyes passes to the right hemisphere and from the right visual field to the left hemisphere. This has been demonstrated in the study of split brain patients who have no connections between the two hemispheres. If they are shown an object to the left eye only, they cannot say what it is because speech centres are in the left hemisphere. The visual cortex

This second paragraph provides some details of the visual pathways but then moves on to consider the visual cortex. Information on the latter is *outside the requirements of this question and therefore would receive no credit*.

contains individual cells that respond to lines of a particular orientation. This was demonstrated in a study by Hubel and Wiesel in 1962, research which was awarded the Nobel Prize. They placed microelectrodes in certain cells and then showed various lines to cats. When a line of a particular orientation was shown to the cat, the brain cell fired. They also found complex and hypercomplex cells which responded to combinations of lines. This research is unethical because it damages the brains of the animals used in the research. It also may not be generalisable to humans.

So far I have described the structure of the visual system. Its function is clearly to see but vision is more than just recording data, it involves processing sensory data and there are many ways that this is achieved even at the retina. Take lateral inhibition for example. When any photosensitive cell is stimulated, it inhibits activity in surrounding cells. The result is that the borders between light and dark things are emphasised and this enables us to see edges of objects. Another retinal form of visual processing is sensory adaptation. This happens when you have been in the dark and come into a brightly lit room, the light then appears brighter for a while. The same is true when you are in a very bright light. In both cases the eye has to adapt to the new conditions which is partly related to the pupil changing size and also to producing more photopigment. All of these processes are important means of ensuring accurate perception.

Colour perception also takes place at the retina. The trichromatic theory proposes that there are three types of cone: red-, green- and blue-sensitive ones. Colour perception is a consequence of mixing signals from each receptor and is supported by evidence of only three types of cone pigment. However, this theory can not explain why it is so rare to find green-blue colour blindness nor can it explain negative afterimages. The opponent-process theory can explain these, and this can be combined with the trichromatic theory. The opponent cells (red-green, blue-yellow and black-white) work in opposition. It is probable that the three cone types of the trichromatic theory send signals to opponent cells, and this produces the perception of colour.

15/24

How to score full marks

Answer the question set

- The candidate clearly knows a lot but has **failed to select the right information** for this question. From the examiner's viewpoint it is not clear if Jack actually does know more than this or whether he has simply not been selective. **Marks can only be awarded for the material on the page.** Remember, **it is not simply what you know but how you use it**.

- For full marks Jack should have **omitted the material on the visual cortex** and could have provided **more detail about the visual pathways**. For example, he could have given information about the LGN (lateral geniculate nucleus), one located on each side of the thalamus and each of which contains six layers of cells, three from each retina. He could also have mentioned the superior colliculus, which receives input from ganglion cells and may be linked to the phenomenon of blindsight, where individuals who are blind due to damage in the visual cortex can nevertheless sometimes reach for objects.

Learn to summarise your knowledge effectively

- You only have 30 minutes to write your response to the question and **may often have much more to say than can possibly be written in this time**. Do not assume that you will suddenly be able to select the important facts when writing your exam response. **Practise the art of summarising (précis) beforehand**. Distilling your knowledge in this way should also be an **effective aid to making the material more memorable**.

Provide sufficient AO2 material

- This is generally a problem for exam candidates and especially problematic when the question involves biological systems. **How do you find suitable commentary** in such cases? The most obvious source is the use of research studies. You can then offer **criticisms of the methodology** of these studies, but such criticism should **challenge the validity of the findings** rather than being a general consideration of the study.

- A further means of evaluation would be to consider **applications of the knowledge** presented. In the case of the visual system this knowledge might be used to understand and/or treat damage to the visual system.

- Biological systems can also be evaluated by considering **situations when the system does not work, or works anomalously**, as in the case of blindsight. In addition, you can provide evaluation through any form of commentary which **establishes the value of the knowledge**. Jack has done this at the end of the third paragraph by saying 'All of these processes are important means of ensuring accurate perception'.

- It would also be creditworthy to **consider alternative explanations**, such as the role of experience on the visual system. This is illustrated in a study by Banks et al. (1975), who looked at children born with squint eyesight, a condition where the two eyes do not co-ordinate properly. The effect of this is that the input from the eyes (binocular vision) does not match, which limits visual precision. The defect can be corrected with an operation. However, Banks et al. found that, if this wasn't done before the age of 4, such children suffered permanently impaired binocular vision.

Question to try

Question 1

Describe and evaluate **two or more** explanations of divided attention.　　　[24 marks]

[Time allowed: 30 minutes]

Exam Questions

Time allowed: 30 minutes

Question 1

(a) Describe **one** theory of cognitive development. [12 marks]

(b) Evaluate this theory with reference to alternative explanations. [12 marks]

Question 2

Discuss research into the formation of identity in adolescence. [24 marks]

Question 3

Discuss research into cognitive changes in late adulthood. [24 marks]

How to 'deconstruct' a question and plan an effective answer

This section deals with Question 1 above.

Mark allocation

● In this question the two skills, **AO1** (knowledge and understanding) and **AO2** (analysis and evaluation), are separated into part (a) and part (b). Part (a) requires you to present a description of **one** theory of cognitive development. **Half the marks** for the question are available for this part, so you must spend **half of the time** (i.e. 15 minutes). You may feel you have more to write for part (a) than part (b) and thus aim to write more to achieve a higher mark. However, your time would be **much better spent trying to get more marks for part (b)**. Maximise marks in part (a) by providing a description of your theory which has **depth and breadth**. In other words, provide some details but do not write a list of facts (breadth). You should try to give a rounded description of the theory (depth).

● In part (a) you must **only describe one theory** and save other theories for part (b), where you are required to evaluate the original theory in terms of alternative approaches. **This does not mean describing other theories.** You must **use your knowledge effectively** to highlight similarities and differences between theory (a) and other approaches. Such contrasts serve as a commentary and highlight the value of theory (a).

● You may also offer **other forms of evaluation** because the question only requires you to 'make reference to' alternative theories in your evaluation. This means that you **must** make reference to alternative theories **but other forms of evaluation will also be creditworthy**. You might, for example, use research evidence that either **supports and/or challenges** theory (a). Further evaluation could be provided by looking at useful **applications** of the theory.

Planning your response

● Three theories of cognitive development are named in the specification: Piaget, Vygotsky and information processing theory. Whichever one you select, **you must ensure that you can**

describe different aspects of the theory. For Piaget's theory, do not simply list the ages and stages because this would be a **limited account**.

● In part (b) you could get full marks for using just alternative explanations as your evaluation, but it might be better to **consider other means of evaluation**. If you choose to mention research studies you must ensure (as with the theories) that **you do not describe this material more than absolutely necessary but use it as a means of evaluation**.

● **Identify the constituent elements** of the essay and use these to guide the **essay structure**. Good structure communicates **clear knowledge and understanding**:

  ■ **Part (a):** This part should contain about 300 words and take 15 minutes.
    Paragraph 1: Outline the essence of the theory you've selected.
    Paragraph 2: Describe a key aspect of the theory.
    Paragraph 3: Describe a second key aspect of the theory.

  ■ **Part (b):** This part should contain about 300 words and take 15 minutes. If you try to cover the four paragraphs below, each one must be short yet 'coherently elaborated'.
    Paragraph 4: Identify an alternative theory and use it to establish some strengths and/or weaknesses of your first theory.
    Paragraph 5: Identify a second alternative theory.
    Paragraph 6: Consider the extent to which the theory is/is not supported by studies.
    Paragraph 7: Consider the practical application of the theory.

◎ Paragraph 1

● Begin by identifying some **key principles** of the theory.

  ■ Piaget proposed that thinking in children is not simply a change due to gaining more knowledge (a quantitative change) but that there are **important qualitative differences between child and adult thinking**.

  ■ Such changes occur largely through **maturation**. This makes Piaget's theory a **biological** theory. Biological **readiness** is the prerequisite for change.

◎ Paragraph 2

● An appropriate approach would be to look at the features of learning.

  ■ Infants are born with innate **schema** (reflexes). These schema are changed when the infant experiences something that does not fit existing schema. Such a mismatch creates **disequilibrium** and this drives the learning process.

  ■ Piaget used the term **accommodation** to describe the process of generating new schema to fit new experiences. He used the term **assimilation** to describe how the child (or any learner) deals with experiences that fit existing schema.

◎ Paragraph 3

● The most memorable feature of Piaget's theory is 'ages and stages'.

  ■ In the first stage of development innate sensory and motor schema are co-ordinated so the infant learns to **match sensations and motor actions** and co-ordinate what he/she can do. The idea of 'circular reactions' is that the infant repeats certain behaviours over and over again to achieve this co-ordination.

  ■ During the second year the child starts to cope with **abstract concepts**, chiefly understanding and producing language.

  ■ Piaget termed the next stage '**pre-operational**', referring to the fact that children between the ages of 2 and 7 do not think logically. Operations are like the rules of arithmetic; they are internally consistent. A characteristic behaviour of this stage is lack of ability to conserve. The child is 'fooled' by the appearance of things.

- In the next stages, the **ability to think logically** develops first only in concrete situations (the **concrete operational** stage) and later in abstract situations (the stage of **formal operations**).

Paragraph 4

- You are now ready to begin part (b) and evaluate Piaget's theory. For high marks you must **demonstrate that you are well informed and can elaborate the points you make**. You must also be **highly selective** and **avoid description**.

  - Vygotsky's theory placed greater emphasis on **social influences**.
  - Piaget agreed that learning is enhanced if the 'teacher' presents a child with **situations which challenge existing schema** (i.e. ones where the existing schema do not fit new experience). But Piaget believed that this would only work when the child is ready.
  - Vygotsky suggested that learning only happens when an 'expert' leads the child through the **zone of proximal development**. Piaget argued that children learn without social input.

Paragraph 5

- You should also be familiar with information processing approaches so it may be worthwhile to briefly contrast these with Piaget's theory.

  - Information processing theorists such as Case also suggest that some of cognitive development is related to maturation. Case proposed that an important factor is the **myelinisation of neurons** which increases the speed of nervous transmission.
  - Children appear to think more quickly as they get older because they also learn about learning and develop metacognitive skills such as **categorisation**.

Paragraph 6

- Useful AO2 marks can be gained through considering the research evidence. You must focus on **coherent elaboration** of a few points rather than brief mention of more material.

  - An important way to establish the value of a theory is to **consider whether it is supported by research evidence**. Subsequent studies of conservation (e.g. Samuel and Bryant) showed that asking two questions may confuse young children.
  - However, this only suggests that Piaget may have got the actual ages wrong but does not challenge the **sequence of development** that is the key to his theory. It may be that children are developing earlier today – which is what Vygotsky's theory would suggest as a consequence of being immersed in a more knowledgeable culture.
  - Other research (e.g. Freund 1990) has shown that practice and working with experts (peers or adults) leads to improved performance. Piaget claimed that practice shouldn't enhance development, though he did suggest this would occur when a child is ready.

Paragraph 7

- At this point you might have run out of time, so may only discuss applications briefly.

  - An important way to establish the value of Piaget's theory is in terms of its usefulness in education. His views on **active** rather than **passive** learning and on the importance of readiness have shaped primary education in the UK.

ROSIE'S ANSWER TO QUESTION 2

Discuss research into the formation of identity in adolescence.

[24 marks]

Adolescence has been called a time of storm and stress. It is a stressful time for parents and teenagers. There are a number of different theories about adolescence, some of which support this view of storm and stress and others that suggest it need not be like this.

The first theory I will look at is Erikson's psychodynamic account. Erikson suggested that at each stage of development there are psychosocial crises that have to be successfully resolved for healthy psychological development. The crisis for adolescence is to resolve the conflict between identity and role confusion. Before adolescence the child had a sense of identity, but this is challenged by the physical changes of puberty. The adolescent experiences role confusion relating to job choices as well as more decisions about what personal beliefs to hold. Erikson felt that it was an important part of becoming an adult to commit to a set of roles in life. Resolution of this role confusion results in formation of an adult identity. In order to do this the adolescent engages in psychosocial moratorium, a kind of rest period during which time the adolescent adopts certain attitudes or occupations temporarily in order to decide which suits them best. Role-sampling is a way of establishing one's own identity, the dominant task for this age group.

One criticism of this approach is that Erikson's idea that identity formation is related to role-decisions may be out of date. Erikson was also criticised because his theory was difficult to test.

The first paragraph *contributes* very *little* to the essay in general though it does give it some structure. *Any introduction should be no longer than this.*

This is a *competent* and *clear* description of Erikson's theory, communicating *knowledge* and *understanding*. The material is *relevant* since the theory is strongly related to the formation of identity, but it is a shame that Rosie *has not more specifically addressed* 'identity'. As it stands it makes one feel that she is just reiterating a prepared answer rather than *genuinely trying to address the question set*. Some small changes could have made all the difference, such as, 'Erikson suggests that identity is formed...'.

A very *weak commentary* on Erikson's theory which shows *little evidence of elaboration*. Rosie might have explained each point, for example that the theory is out of date because people are now less committed to the idea of a job for life. She might also have included some positive criticisms.

Marcia developed another theory, extending Erikson's idea. The advantage of Marcia's approach was that it was devised as a theory that could be tested empirically. First of all Marcia interviewed adolescents about their attitudes and beliefs about a number of different topics such as occupation, religion, politics, and attitudes about sex. He found that interviewees gave one of four kinds of answer reflecting four possible states of adolescence. These states or statuses were:

- Identity diffusion or confusion where the individual hasn't even started to think about the issues.

- Identity foreclosure where an adolescent has prematurely formed an opinion not based on individual consideration.

- Identity moratorium, when decisions about identity are put on hold while the adolescent tries out various roles.

- Identity achievement when the period of crisis is passed and the adolescent has achieved his/her own identity.

This scheme enables researchers to see what stage different adolescents are at and associate this with individual factors. For example, Waterman (1985) studied people aged 11–21 and found a decrease in diffusion status and an increase in identity achievement with age. Moratorium was quite uncommon at all ages. Waterman (1982) also found that domineering parenting is associated with identity foreclosure whereas moratorium and identity achievement are connected with a more warm, democratic style.

A rather different approach was taken by Coleman (1974) who argued that most adolescents do not experience severe difficulties. They tend to focus on particular problems at particular times and thus avoid conflict and stress. This theory was called the focal theory because of this idea of focusing on something. Some adolescents may experience stress because they have too many problems at one time but this is no more likely than at any other time. This view is supported by research by Coleman and Hendry (1990) who interviewed 800 teenage boys and girls. They found that typical issues such as self-image, being alone, occupational choice, and sexual and parental relationships all peaked at different ages.

The final explanation is good because it presents a *contrast* but its *relevance to the question* of the formation of identity is not clear. This reinforces the view that the essay is a *prepared one* and Rosie has made no effort to *adapt her knowledge to the question set*, a very common failing that *loses important marks*.

Rutter et al.'s (1976) study of thousands of adolescents living on the Isle of Wight also found little stress at this time of life. Where there were psychiatric problems these had mostly been ongoing since childhood, but in cases where problems did first appear in adolescence there were often family problems which may have acted as a stressor.

14/24

How to score full marks

Answer the question set

- This is an instruction that is frequently given to students but is all too often disregarded. The rationale is simple. If examiners credited material that was not directly relevant to the question set you could simply prepare 10 or so essays and use one in the examination. There would be no need for you to cover the specification. In order to sample your knowledge effectively the examiner sets a (fairly predictable) question but intends you to **address that question** rather than give an answer you prepared earlier. You might be very lucky and find a question that is just right for you, but do **attend carefully to the specific requirements of the question rather than answering the question you wanted to see**.

Offer coherent elaboration of commentary

- One of the criteria for AO2 marks is **coherent elaboration**. This enables the examiner to distinguish between a candidate who has some knowledge of critical issues but doesn't fully understand them and the candidate who has a clear understanding and can **explain** the criticism or comment that is being made. **Explanation amounts to coherent elaboration**. To achieve high marks, **state your point and then explain or elaborate it**.

Balance your answer

- Rosie's answer is weakest in the AO2 material, and this would decrease the overall mark. **It is not sufficient at advanced level to learn a set of facts and describe these carefully**. You must be able to **demonstrate the value of this knowledge** by using research evidence and other forms of commentary (such as consideration of applications, or strengths and weaknesses of the research described, or consequences). **Assessment objective 2 concerns your opinion – not just a 'commonsense' opinion but one that is informed by psychological study, theory and application**.

- **You must ensure that you give AO2 as much attention as AO1.** It is the AO1 marks that candidates find easiest and the AO2 marks are generally lower. Rosie needed to have more material to use for evaluation and to be able to elaborate this material.

Question to try

Question 3

Discuss research into cognitive changes in late adulthood.   [24 marks]

[Time allowed: 30 minutes]

Examiner's hints

- 'Discuss' is an AO1 and AO2 term. Therefore, for AO1 you must **describe** research into cognitive changes in late adulthood and then, for AO2, you need to **assess** this research. 'Research' refers to either **theories** or **studies**.

- You may divide your answer clearly into AO1 and AO2, so that all the description is presented first and all the evaluation is considered last. However, it is preferable to **embed at least some of the commentary** in the essay as you go along so that you describe a research study or a theory and then offer assessment of it.

- Such assessment might be in terms of **studies and/or theories** or, if you are assessing a study, you might consider **methodological or ethical issues** that challenge the validity of the research. If you are considering a theory, assessment might be in terms of **logical flaws or useful applications** of this knowledge. **Any form of commentary** may be credited as AO2 as long as it is **psychologically based**.

- You might be tempted to simply plunge in and start describing research. However, it would be advisable to **spend a short time planning a structure for your essay** so that you 'tell a story' rather than provide a list of research. Such structure receives **credit** within the **AO1** marking criteria. One way to structure an essay would be to consider different areas of cognitive behaviour, such as intelligence and memory.

- You might end the essay with some commentary on general issues related to cognitive changes, such as the **application** of such research.

Exam Questions

Time allowed: 30 minutes

Question 1

Outline and evaluate **two** biological explanations of apparent altruism in non-human animals.   [24 marks]

Question 2

Describe and evaluate research into animal language.   [24 marks]

Question 3

Discuss how **one or more** human mental disorders might be explained from an evolutionary perspective.   [24 marks]

How to 'deconstruct' a question and plan an effective answer

This section deals with Question 1 above.

🎯 Mark allocation

● This question requires you to demonstrate two skills, **AO1** (knowledge and understanding) and **AO2** (analysis and evaluation). These are indicated by the 'injunctions' used in the question. In this case, the word '**outline**' is the AO1 term and the word '**evaluate**' is the AO2 term. **Half** the available marks are for the AO1 content of the answer, and **half** for the AO2 content. If your answer fails to address **both** of these skills, or provides them in a very unbalanced way, **you will lose the opportunity to pick up the marks available** for that component. No matter how good the AO1 content, the maximum mark is still only 12 if no AO2 evaluation is present. **It is important that you understand exactly the requirements of this question**. It asks for **two** explanations (not one or more than two), so presenting a general response that does not focus on two explanations in particular misses the point of the question.

🎯 Planning your response

● **Altruism** can be defined as an act of helping which increases the (reproductive) fitness of the individual who is helped, at some cost to the fitness of the helper. The essential cost and benefit at stake here is **fitness**, which is a measure of reproductive success. Helping a close relative or one of their offspring can be considered to be an example of a selfish commitment to maximising **inclusive fitness**, which is why this is known as **apparent altruism**.

● There are 30 minutes allowed for this question, so you can divide your answer into four convenient 7.5-minute 'chunks' (each one about 150 words):

1   An **outline** (i.e. a **summary description**) of the first biological explanation of apparent altruism.
2   An **evaluation** of the first biological explanation of altruism.
3   An **outline** of the second biological explanation of apparent altruism.
4   An **evaluation** of the second biological explanation of apparent altruism.

Paragraph 1

- With questions such as this, where there are very **specific** requirements, **it is important to start earning marks straight away**. The question **does not ask you to define** altruism (it is safe to assume you understand what it is) but to **outline explanations** of altruism. This first paragraph, therefore, should contain a summary of your first selected explanation. You might, for example, choose **kin selection** (i.e. individuals act favourably towards others to whom they are genetically related), so you should outline the main points of that explanation here, e.g.

  - Some behaviours, although they may reduce the survival chances or reproductive effectiveness of an **individual** animal, serve to increase the likelihood of the individual's close **genetic relatives** surviving and reproducing.
  - It is possible for an altruistic individual to **pass on more copies of its genes** through helping genetic relatives survive and subsequently reproduce than would be possible from direct offspring alone.
  - The reproductive gain from an individual's own offspring (a measure of its **direct fitness**) plus the reproductive gain from non-descendent genetic relatives (a measure of **indirect fitness**) together make up the individual's **inclusive fitness**.
  - For kin selection to be effective, animals must 'know' those with whom they share genes so that they might favour those over non-relatives. Possible mechanisms for this include **spatial proximity** (family groups tend to stay together) and **phenotype matching** (related individuals have certain characteristics such as smell, appearance or behaviour in common).

Paragraph 2

- Although there is no golden rule about the order in which you should attempt questions such as this, following the descriptive content with evaluative commentary is one acceptable route. **Remember that evaluation is far more than simply 'criticising' an explanation.** It also includes looking for supporting research evidence, and **assessing the overall 'worth' of the explanation**. Appropriate evaluative content might include the following:

  - There are a number of reasons why it is important for an individual to respond differently to kin and non-kin. Parents who fail to recognise their own offspring would **waste resources** on another's young. Related individuals who collaborate are more likely to **fend off aggression** from others who are non-relatives.
  - Evidence for the importance of phenotype matching comes from studies of **Belding's ground squirrels**. Females raised with full and half-sisters consistently show more altruistic behaviour towards their full sisters than their half-sisters.
  - Studies of **mate choice** in different strains of inbred mice have supported the claim that genetically similar individuals share distinctive odours that serve both to elicit altruistic behaviour and also prevent inbreeding.

Paragraph 3

- At this point you should be half-way through your answer, and ready to begin a summary description of the second explanation of altruism, which might be **reciprocal altruism**.

  - Trivers (1971) argued that one animal might show altruistic behaviour towards another if the recipient of this favour **reciprocated** some time in the future.
  - Research has found that **unrelated vampire bats** regurgitate food for one another on their return to the nesting site. These activities between unrelated individuals tend to be reciprocated, i.e. they build up a relationship based upon mutual exchanges of favour.
  - Reciprocal altruism may only evolve in species where individuals could **recognise** each other and **apply sanctions** to those who refused to reciprocate.

- Axelrod and Hamilton (1981) proposed that cheating in reciprocal arrangements might be prevented by the use of a **'tit for tat' strategy** which would **reward co-operation and discourage defection.**

◎ Paragraph 4

- If you have managed to keep to your timing, you should now be ready to embark on the final paragraph which, for the purposes of this illustration, is an evaluation of the reciprocal altruism explanation. Appropriate content might include:

  - In the case of the vampire bats, all bats benefit from the 'insurance policy' of being fed by others in times of need. Those who have donated food in the past will be better placed to receive it when they are in need. **Co-operation in the long term is thus the strategy that best serves the selfish interests of each individual.**

  - The 'tit for tat' strategy has two major advantages. It is **retaliatory** – animals who 'cheat' on this reciprocal arrangement by not returning the favour would face the consequences of the altruist refusing to help them in the future. It is **conciliatory** – animals do not miss out on the future benefits of co-operation by holding a grudge against an animal that had once defected.

  - A problem with explaining how this form of altruism has evolved concerns the **time period between giving and receiving**. Until the altruist has been repaid, the altruist has gained nothing. In fact, it is worse off than if it had done nothing. This may well explain why documented cases of reciprocal altruism are rare.

MARK'S ANSWER TO QUESTION 3

Discuss how **one or more** human mental disorders might be explained from an evolutionary perspective. [24 marks]

Depression is a very common mental disorder. There are two main types of depression — unipolar depression and bipolar depression. Unipolar depression is the more common of the two forms of depression, and is characterised by a number of symptoms, including a sad, depressed mood, difficulties in sleeping, and thoughts of death or suicide. A second type of mental disorder is phobias. Phobias are a type of anxiety disorder where there is a persistent fear of an object or situation. As a result of this fear, people who suffer from a phobia will try to avoid the object of their fear as that way they can avoid the anxiety associated with it. Examples of phobias include agoraphobia, which is a fear of open spaces, and arachnophobia, which is a fear of snakes. Having a phobia tends to make it difficult for a person to lead a normal life.

The rank theory of depression suggests that depression might be an adaptive response rather than a maladaptive one. If one of our ancestors were to lose a fight over a resource, it would be profitable for them to break off from the fight to lick their wounds. In this way they would have time to recover and would be able to fight another day. This means that they would minimise the risk of further injury. Rank theory proposes that depression has evolved as an involuntary process which prevents the individual from continuing the fight by giving them a lack of confidence and a lack of energy, both characteristics of clinical depression. Over time, depression might be triggered by any sort of loss (such as bereavement or divorce) rather than being restricted to a loss of status.

Phobias can be explained by looking at the type of environment in which the fears they represent might have been relevant. Agoraphobia might have developed because it was dangerous to wander too far away from the home territory, and arachnophobia might have developed because poisonous snakes would have been far more common in our ancestors' day. As with the rank theory of depression described earlier, having a fear response towards these things would be adaptive, as someone with a fear of open spaces would not have wandered too far away from their home and therefore would not be as vulnerable from predators and other humans. Claustrophobia might also have developed for the same reasons. It would be difficult to escape from a confined space (such as a cave), so people who avoided such spaces were more likely to survive.

The rank theory of depression is a good theory because it shows how what we now see as maladaptive behaviour (being clinically depressed) could actually have had a more adaptive function when it first developed. Some psychologists believe that we try too hard to explain the things that have gone wrong in a mental disorder (e.g. brain damage or neurotransmitter malfunction) without looking at the reason why the disorder might have developed in the first place. The same is true of anxiety disorders. It is quite normal to be fearful in situations that are dangerous for us. Indeed, not to be anxious in those situations would be abnormal. The fact that evolution 'prepares' us for potentially dangerous situations by making it easier to acquire a fear of them makes it more likely that we will survive when faced with them. The fact that we tend to have phobias of things that are not really significant nowadays simply overlooks the fact that they were extremely significant millions of years ago when they first developed.

13/24

How to score full marks

Don't waste time

- For whatever reason, students frequently begin answers to questions such as this by **offering material which is going to get them few, if any, marks**. Sometimes this is a 'security blanket' and gives students a gentle way into the answer. Sometimes, as may be the case with Mark's answer, students feel they will lose marks if they fail to define all terms and display all appropriate knowledge. **It is always wise to 'deconstruct' each question carefully before putting pen to paper, and work out what will and what will not gain marks.** Marks are only awarded for material that is **explicitly relevant to the question set**, which here means material that offers the **explanation** of mental disorders from an evolutionary perspective. Of course having an understanding of the nature of depression and phobias, and the symptoms that make up these disorders, is important, but this is **not** the section on psychopathology. **Stick to the specific requirements of the question, and make sure you access the marks the examiner has available to give you.**

Engage and elaborate

- It is very easy to lose sight of the requirements of the question, and get side-tracked along the way. Mark has shown in the final paragraph that he understands the logic behind the evolutionary perspective of mental disorders, but this understanding is not that apparent in the middle two paragraphs. He shows **why** such behaviour might have been advantageous to our ancestors yet fails to build on that by explaining **how** such behaviour would have been 'selected' by natural selection and perpetuated to the present day. Remember that the question asks for an explanation of modern-day behaviours, not a justification of ancestral ones. **When you have so few words to express your answer, it is wise to choose them carefully**. In order to **engage effectively** with the question, you must **elaborate only those points that have an important role in its answer.**

Balance your answer

- Although some areas of the specification appear less amenable to critical evaluation than others (with comparative being a case in point), there is always scope for **good critical commentary**. This should not be overlooked, or even treated as an afterthought. **Remember** (Mark seems to have forgotten this) **that there is exactly the same number of marks available for the AO2 content as there is for the AO1 content**.

- Mark's response to this question seems simply to suffer from **bad planning**, as he has spent **too much time getting into the essay** (paragraph 1) and **too little time** (paragraph 4) **offering the critical appraisal that earns the AO2 marks**. Overall, an answer like this would receive about 7 marks for AO1 and about 6 marks for AO2, giving 13 marks overall, which is equivalent to a Grade C.

Question to try

Question 2

Describe and evaluate research into animal language. [24 marks]

[Time allowed: 30 minutes]

Exam Questions

Time allowed: 40 minutes

Question 1

Discuss evidence for and against the existence of culture-bound syndromes.

[30 marks]

Question 2

'Research evidence suggests that schizophrenia has a genetic basis; but concordance rates in identical twins are not 100%. This means that genetic explanations alone are insufficient.'

With reference to the above quotation, discuss explanations of schizophrenia.

[30 marks]

Question 3

Compare and contrast any **two** therapies used to treat mental disorders.   [30 marks]

How to 'deconstruct' a question and plan an effective answer

This section deals with Question 3 above.

Mark allocation

- On Unit 5 answers (as compared with Unit 4 answers) you have **extra time** and **extra marks** (an extra 10 minutes and an extra 6 marks, divided equally between AO1 and AO2). There is also an **additional marking criteria: the synoptic criteria**. This means that, when you write an essay on individual differences, you will be assessed for this criteria as well as all the usual ones used in Unit 4 for AO1 and AO2.

- The injunction '**compare and contrast**' is both an **AO1** and AO2 term requiring you to describe two therapies (i.e. AO1) and then compare them with each other, highlighting similarities and differences (this is the AO2 element). The term 'compare and contrast' indicates that you can and should do both – compare **and** contrast. In this question, as in all questions, there is an **equal number of marks for each assessment objective**. You need to focus on providing descriptions of each therapy (AO1) and then attracting AO2 marks from the compare/contrast part of the essay.

- As always, you must respond **exactly** to the requirements of this question. It asks for **two therapies** only. These may both be examples of behavioural therapies (such as systematic desensitisation and flooding) or they may be two more contrasting and 'more global' therapies (such as behavioural therapy and psychoanalysis). **You must cover two therapies** in order to offer comparisons. There is no partial performance possibility (i.e. 9/15 marks if only one therapy is described).

- All essays on Unit 5 are assessed in terms of synopticity as well as the other criteria used in Unit 4. Synopticity and the synoptic criteria are discussed in the introduction of this book.

- These are some ideas about what synoptic material you might include when writing an essay on treating mental disorders. AO1 material (description) is on the left and AO2 material (evaluation/commentary) is on the right.

> Biological therapies come in a variety of forms, including drug treatments, electroconvulsive therapies (ECT) and psychosurgery.

> **Each of these therapies has specific situations where they may be the most appropriate form of treatment.**

> The use of biological therapies raises various ethical issues, such as those relating to informed consent.

> **However, informed consent may be an unrealistic ideal in relation to mental disorders as patients may not be in a position to make such decisions.**

> The use of behavioural therapies raises the issue of social control.

> **Who decides what behaviours are desirable or undesirable? In the history of humankind there have been instances where psychiatry has been a force for social control, as in the case of homosexuality and Russian dissidents.**

> It is difficult to measure the effectiveness of psychoanalytic treatment because there are so many variables involved and this makes it difficult to conduct a controlled and statistically valid outcome study.

> **On the other hand, this may be the only means of making comparisons between different therapies and offering information to prospective patients and their families.**

Planning your response

- Which therapies should you write about? It is desirable to **select broad categories**, such as behavioural therapy, rather than narrow ones such as social skills training because this gives you more material to draw on and provides you with a variety of different aspects of the therapy for comparisons to be made.

- There are several ways that you might organise your response to this essay. One way would be to **describe therapy 1 and then describe therapy 2**. This would cover the AO1 content of your essay. The second half of the essay would then focus on comparisons and contrasts between them.

- Alternatively you might **embed the AO2** by describing one aspect of therapy 1 and comparing this with a similar aspect of therapy 2. Thus you would simultaneously cover AO1 and AO2. You would continue to do this for other aspects of the therapies.

- There are 40 minutes allowed for this question, in which time it is likely that you could write about 800 words. If you take the first approach described above, then the first half of the essay might be subdivided into two chunks, each of 200 words and each describing the therapy. The second half of the essay might be divided into four chunks, each of 100 words and each examining a point of comparison or contrast. This means you would cover four points of comparison/contrast.

- If you take the second approach described above, the essay could be divided into six chunks or paragraphs, each of about 150 words and approximately 6 minutes of writing time. Each paragraph would cover one aspect of the therapies.

- If we take this second approach, the essay might be structured as follows.

Paragraph 1

- There is no requirement for an elegant introduction but you might feel more comfortable stating some **basic descriptive material** at the outset which also **establishes the structure** for the essay (organisation is one of the AO1 criteria).

  - Two of the most common and successful forms of therapy are behaviour therapy (based on both classical and operant conditioning) and biological (somatic) therapy.
  - **Behaviour therapies** assume that mental disorders are the result of **faulty learning**, i.e. they are due to nurture.
  - **Biological therapies** draw on **genetic** and **physiological** explanations. It may be that the susceptibility for a particular disorder is inherited or it may be that some life experience has led to a hormonal imbalance, as in the case of postnatal depression related to hormonal changes after birth. Therefore this is both a **nurture and nature** view.

Paragraph 2

- In each of the next five paragraphs one further point of comparison needs to be examined, each time incorporating material that is descriptive (AO1) as well as evaluative (AO2). In this paragraph you could consider the synoptic issue of determinism.

  - Both of these approaches to therapy are **deterministic**.
  - Behaviour therapy is based on the idea that what is learned through reinforcements can be **unlearned** also through reinforcements. Such reinforcements **determine an individual's behaviour** rather than the behaviour being an outcome of self-determination (free will).
  - Biological therapies also assume a **deterministic relationship between causes and behaviours**. For example, schizophrenia may be due to excess of the neurotransmitter dopamine (possibly a genetic cause) and this leads to the use of certain drugs to treat schizophrenia (e.g. phenothiazines). It is assumed that if the imbalance is corrected the disorder is treated. This assumes a simple causal and deterministic relationship.

Paragraph 3

- A further synoptic issue you could consider is reductionism.

  - Both approaches are also **reductionist** insofar as they each reduce behaviour to rather simple components.
  - In the case of behavioural therapies, explanations are reduced to **stimulus-response relationships**. For example, aversion therapy is based on the principle that one can pair an unpleasant stimulus with a maladaptive response and thus create a new stimulus-response link which would prevent an individual continuing the unhealthy behaviour, such as addiction.
  - A biological therapy such as the use of drugs to treat mental disorders is also reductionist because behaviour is reduced to simply **chemical causes** and/or **genetic explanations**.

Paragraph 4

- In paragraphs 2 and 3 you could have covered some similarities. There are also some important differences.

  - Both sorts of therapy have been shown to be **highly successful** but this is especially true for target disorders.
  - Behaviour therapy is especially appropriate for treating phobias. **Systematic desensitisation** was developed by Wolpe to treat fears and anxieties by training a patient to relax through graded exposure to a fearful stimulus. A conditioned fear response is replaced by one of relaxation.
  - Behaviour therapy is less suitable for more psychological rather than behavioural disorders where forms of psychotherapy are more successful, or in some case biological therapies.
  - Drug therapies are not often used for phobias but they are common in the treatment of **depression** and **schizophrenia**. ECT is also used to treat severe depression and 60–70% of such patients improve (Sackeim et al. 1993).

Paragraph 5

- A further point of contrast you could mention is the **ease of treatment**.

  - Drug therapies have become very popular possibly because they require **little effort** on the part of the patient. Drug therapies have enormous 'costs' in terms of addictions and side effects, yet people are very willing to use them to treat mental disorders. This may be because they are so easy.
  - In contrast behaviour therapies require investment in terms of **time** and **effort**. With systematic desensitisation the patient must be willing to focus on relaxation and willing to return for several sessions. Token economy takes a long time, as does social skills training.

Paragraph 6

- Finally, you could consider a further synoptic issue – ethics.

  - A very important way of evaluating all therapies is in terms of **ethics**. The major ethical issue in relation to behaviour therapies is the one of **control** and **behaviour manipulation**. The therapist shapes the patient's behaviour according to his/her own goals and those of society in general. The patient may not share the same goals (e.g. a school refuser may not wish to change his/her behaviour). To what extent is it acceptable to ignore individual rights? On the other hand, the general public has rights too and also individuals may need protection from self-harm (e.g. anorexia sufferers, who may ultimately kill themselves).
  - Ethics are also an issue in relation to biological therapies in terms of the **potential for harm** from treatments like ECT and psychosurgery, and also drugs. Such chemical straightjackets may not be desirable from the individual's point of view but may be necessary from society's point of view.
  - Both approaches aim to treat the **symptoms** and not always the causes, which is an ethical matter because this may be in the interests of society rather than the individual.

PIP'S ANSWER TO QUESTION 1

Discuss evidence for and against the existence of culture-bound syndromes.
[30 marks]

Culture-bound syndromes (CBSs) are mental disorders that do not fit into currently existing categories as defined by international classification schemes, and they tend to be associated with a particular population or cultural area. The key question is whether certain conditions, such as koro, represent a distinctly different disorder from those known in the 'West' (and included in Western classification schemes) or whether it is actually more or less the same underlying disorder but it is expressed differently in terms of the presenting symptoms. Such symptoms are related to cultural context. An example of this can be seen in one of the symptoms of schizophrenia, which is hearing voices from the television. Such a symptom could not have occurred in a different historical period and the same argument can be put forward when people from a different culture express their illness in different ways.

Koro is worth considering because a distinction is made between true koro and a koro-like state. Koro is a disorder where the individual believes that his penis is retracting into his body, and this will result in death. It is found in Asia and occasional cases have been reported elsewhere. It seems that some cases can be relatively easily treated with reassurance and are definitely cultural in origin (true koro) whereas others (a koro-like state) result in genuine panic and are the result of an underlying universal disorder. This would suggest that koro is a true CBS.

On the other hand, there is the view that the symptoms of even true koro are simply a culturally-relative expression of a universal disorder. In which case we would have the same underlying condition simply expressed differently. Yap has argued that many apparent CBSs are just that. For example, latah (from Malaya) and susto (from Peru) are both brought on by a sudden stimulus, and are simply different cultural expressions of a 'primary fear reaction', a condition recognised by Western classification schemes.

There are three possible explanations for mental illnesses in relation to cultural issues. First that mental illnesses are absolute. This is the view that symptoms and the underlying disorder are the same all over the world. Second, that mental disorders are universal. This means that the underlying condition is constant but the way it is expressed varies culturally. Third, that there are culturally relative conditions that are unique to the culture in terms of the underlying disorder and the symptoms.

The first is unlikely, the second however is quite possible. For example, as mentioned earlier, schizophrenics may today complain of hearing voices on the TV but expressed their disorder differently 100 years ago. Individuals who are depressed in this country exhibit symptoms such as loss of appetite or difficulty sleeping whereas Nigerians who are depressed often complain of burning sensations in the body, crawling sensations in the head or legs, and a feeling that the stomach is bloated with water (Ebigno 1986). Nevertheless Berry et al. conclude that depression is a universal disorder with culturally-relative symptoms. There is particularly strong evidence that schizophrenia is a universal disorder. This is supported by the fact that incidence rates are fairly similar across the world and that the World Health Organisation found a number of symptoms that were commonly found across many countries. Some of the most common symptoms were lack of insight and hallucinations. Neverthless there were local variations.

But this doesn't mean that <u>all</u> culturally different symptoms are expressions of recognised disorders. It is possible that koro is a CBS with no equivalent in DSM or ICD. This is recognised by the fact that such disorders have been added as an appendix to Western classification schemes.

However, Yap thinks that it may be possible, by and large, to subsume all apparently CBSs within established diagnosis. So that witiko is a mixture of depression and anxiety, and susto is apathy, depression and anxiety. Clearly there is as yet no certain answer to the question of whether CBSs exist or not.

Such apparent academic debate has important real-world consequences for the treatment of mental disorders. Clinicians use Western classification systems as a means of diagnosing mental illness. This means that they may misunderstand or dismiss certain culturally-relative disorders. This may well be the case with diagnoses of schizophrenia.

19/30

How to score full marks

Synoptic criteria

- All essays on Unit 5 are marked in the same way as Unit 4 **except there are also synoptic criteria**. All candidates are likely to gain some 'synoptic' credit in this essay because cultural issues are an integral part of the topic, and Pip certainly raises this issue in the last paragraph when considering cultural bias in diagnosis. However, the rest of the essay focuses very much on the question set and has not provided us with much of a **general view of the whole of psychology** which is required for the synoptic criteria.

- Possible ways to do this would have been to **raise other issues**, such as ethics in relation to classification or the reliability/validity of classification schemes. Classification schemes assume a deterministic relationship between underlying disorders and symptoms. Additionally the attempt to reduce all disorders to a simple classification scheme could have been discussed.

Essay construction

- AO1 concerns 'knowledge and understanding' but there are other criteria in addition to this. One of these criteria refers to the way that the essay is constructed. The ability to write a **well-structured essay** reflects the extent to which you are confident about the stipulated topic area and thus it is used as a means of assessing your knowledge. This means that **essay plans** do receive some reward because they **help you construct your essay in a logical manner**. One way to do this is to follow our suggestion to **deconstruct the question and plan your answer**. Pip's essay is somewhat lacking in this logical structure.

Arguments for and against

- When essay titles require you to discuss **arguments for and against** something then you are required to (a) describe the arguments (for AO1 credit) and (b) assess/analyse/evaluate these arguments (for AO2 credit). It is not the case that arguments 'for' are AO1 and arguments 'against' are AO2 **unless** the 'against' arguments are explicitly used as a means of evaluating the 'for' arguments. If you present the 'for' and 'against' arguments as free-standing then they are both AO1. In Pip's essay there is a reasonable balance between describing the arguments and using one as a counterpoint (AO2) to the other. There are also attempts to evaluate the arguments but this might have been extended further, especially with reference to the synoptic areas.

Question to try

Question 2

'Research evidence suggests that schizophrenia has a genetic basis; but concordance rates in identical twins are not 100%. This means that genetic explanations alone are insufficient.'

With reference to the above quotation, discuss explanations of schizophrenia.   [30 marks]

[Time allowed: 40 minutes]

Examiner's hints

● Quotations are included in questions to offer something to get your teeth into. On some occasions there is no specific requirement to address the quotation. It is merely there to try to be helpful in stimulating your discussion. On other occasions, as with this question, you are **required to refer to the quotation** and, if you do not do so, you will lose marks. It is not sufficient merely to start your essay with some passing reference to the quotation but, in order to attract good marks, you should **continue to engage with the quotation throughout your essay**.

● The injunction used is '**discuss**', which is **an AO1 and AO2 term** requiring you to describe explanations and then evaluate them. This may be done sequentially or concurrently.

● The question permits you to discuss **any explanations of schizophrenia**, i.e. biological and/or psychological. You would gain credit for describing any or all of these and then evaluating the ones you have described. This means that you should have a vast amount of knowledge to draw upon and need to work hard at being selective. You may use the quotation to guide you in this. Greater breadth may increase synopticity through the variety of approaches/explanations covered. However, at the same time you may detract from the detail in your answer because you have covered too much and left insufficient time to describe anything in detail, let alone evaluate it. This is the **depth–breadth trade-off. Selectivity and coherent elaboration** are important criteria to remember.

● One approach to evaluation is to evaluate one explanation with another explanation. However, you must ensure that this is done **explicitly** so that the second explanation is genuinely acting as a means of sustained contrast and evaluation.

Exam Questions

Time allowed: 40 minutes

Question 1

With reference to psychological theories and/or research, discuss the view that these offer a gender-biased view of human behaviour. [30 marks]

Question 2

Describe and evaluate arguments for and against the use of animals in psychological research. [30 marks]

Question 3

With reference to at least **two** areas of psychological investigation, discuss the ethics of socially sensitive research. [30 marks]

How to 'deconstruct' a question and plan an effective answer

This section deals with Question 1 above.

Mark allocation

● The word '**discuss**' is **an AO1 and AO2** term requiring you to 'describe' (AO1) and 'evaluate' (AO2). In this question, as in all questions, there is an equal number of marks for each skill. **AO1** is knowledge and understanding and **AO2** is analysis and evaluation. If your answer fails to address **both** of these skills, or provides them in a very **unbalanced** way, you will simply lose the opportunity to pick up the marks available for that component. No matter how good the AO1 content, the maximum mark is still only 15 if no AO2 evaluation is present.

● In both AO1 and AO2 assessments of Unit 5 there are **synoptic criteria.** You will be assessed on your ability to include knowledge (AO1) and critical appreciation (AO2) of **different theoretical perspectives and/or methodological approaches** (see page 12 for a discussion of synopticity). Given the topic of this essay **it would be difficult *not* to be synoptic** as you will be discussing more than one theory (thus demonstrating your understanding of gender bias in these theories) and possibly different research methodologies. In addition, the very topic of your essay (gender bias) is synoptic as it is an overarching issue. Unlike some synoptic questions, therefore, in this question you are **told** what synoptic approach you must take, i.e. you must discuss theories and/or research in terms of their **gender bias**.

● You should note that if you choose to answer this question by focusing on psychological **theories** that might be gender biased, you should include at least **two**. This is evident from the use of the plural 'theories' in the question. Failing to address at least two would reduce the total number of marks you might attain for this question. You are not **required** to answer in terms of research as this is phrased as an **alternative approach to the question**.

🎯 Planning your response

● This is a fairly wide question, but it does call for quite specialist knowledge, and as such should only be attempted if you really feel you know the area. You are being given the opportunity to embed your answer in **either** theories **or** research **or** both. You might choose to look at traditional gender-'biased' theories (e.g. Freud, Kohlberg etc.), or alternative theories (e.g. Gilligan, Bem etc.) or even theories that represent a particular perspective on development (e.g. nature/nurture).

● Alternatively, you might discuss actual **research strategies** such as the problems of the experiment in investigations of gender difference and the increasing use of qualitative methods that is part of the postmodern revolution in psychology. This suggested answer offers a combination of these two approaches. Remember you are also being awarded marks for your critical evaluation of the material **and** your synoptic ability.

● There are 40 minutes allowed for this question, so you could divide your answer up accordingly. One of the themes of this book is that you should plan your 'journey' before setting out, and this answer is no different. You should endeavour to incorporate the following features into your answer.

  ■ A description of the **assumptions** made within your chosen theories (or research methodologies) that make them gender biased.
  ■ **Commentary** on these theories (or research methodologies) in relation to these assumptions (i.e. not a general evaluation of the theory), including reference to relevant issues/debates (**synoptic AO1**) as well as a commentary on them (**synoptic AO2**).

🎯 Synoptic signposts

● All essays on Unit 5 are assessed in terms of synopticity as well as the other criteria used in Unit 4. Synopticity and the synoptic criteria are discussed in the introduction of this book.

● These are some ideas about what synoptic material you might include when writing an essay on gender bias in psychological theories. AO1 material (description) is on the left and AO2 material (evaluation/commentary) is on the right.

Kohlberg's theory of moral development represents women as morally less developed than men (an alpha bias).

Gilligan challenged Kohlberg's theory with the claim that women have a different moral voice, one based on an ethic of care and responsibility rather than the 'male' ethic of justice and rights.

The 'discovery' of pre-menstrual syndrome has led to a burgeoning of experimental research in this area (Nicolson 1997).

Nicolson argues that many of the differences traditionally identified between pre-menstrual women and others were products of poor research design.

The young boy's identification with his father leads to the formation of a superego and of high moral standards. Girls cannot develop their superego to the same degree as boys.

Critics of Freudian psychoanalysis criticise its culture-bound sexism. Friedan (1965) condemns Freud's account of women on the grounds that he was a 'prisoner of his own culture'.

Paragraph 1

● As a rough estimate of how you might approach this question, this suggested answer is based on a plan of **seven** paragraphs, each one requiring about 5 minutes of writing time. This then allows a further **5** minutes in total for reading, thinking, planning, daydreaming or whatever else you like to do during an examination! In this first paragraph you could set the scene for the theories you are going to discuss by **defining** the nature of gender bias and of the alpha/beta bias distinction in particular.

- **Gender bias** refers to the treatment of men and women in psychological research and theory such as to offer a view that might not justifiably be seen as representing the characteristics of either one of these genders.
- **Alpha-biased theories** are theories that see **real differences** between men and women, and may represent either an **enhancement** or **undervaluing** of one gender compared with the other.
- **Beta-biased theories** tend to **ignore** or **minimise differences** between men and women, either by ignoring questions about the lives of women, or by assuming that findings from studies of males apply equally well to females.
- Most psychological theories tend to lean more towards the beta bias because, in attempting to represent males and females in an objective and unbiased manner, they fail to represent the characteristics of one sex (usually women).

Paragraph 2

● In this second paragraph, you should begin to bring in **theories** that you consider to be gender biased, but do this in such a way that your discussion is **informed** rather than simply being speculative about the bias inherent in a theory. This paragraph has two functions. First, it identifies Kohlberg's theory of moral development as an example of an **alpha bias** theory, and explains **why** this is so. Second, it incorporates **criticism** from Gilligan who takes issue with Kohlberg's views on moral development. As the **synoptic** element of the answer has been predefined, this also serves a synoptic function for both AO1 and AO2 skills.

- **Kohlberg's** theory of moral development (Kohlberg 1976) is typically seen as an example of an alpha bias theory that **undervalues** women, representing them as typically morally less developed than men.
- When scored on Kohlbergian dilemmas, typical female responses that emphasised caring and personal relationships would merit a Stage 3 classification, placing them at a lower level of moral reasoning than men who were often scored at Stage 5.
- **Gilligan's** theory of moral development in women (Gilligan 1977), on the other hand, is an alpha bias theory that **enhances** rather than undervalues women.
- Gilligan challenged Kohlberg's theory with the claim that women have a different moral voice, one based on an ethic of care and responsibility rather than the 'male' ethic of justice and rights.

Paragraph 3

● Although offering a critical stance to Kohlberg's perspective on moral development, Gilligan's theory should also be criticised in order to maximise the AO2 marks available for this question. This third paragraph gives you the opportunity to do just that. On completion of this paragraph, you might reflect (briefly!) on what you have achieved so far. Two theories described and evaluated in terms of their gender bias, and the synoptic requirement of the question has also been addressed. Provided your **time management** is okay, you are on course for an effective answer to this question.

- Critics of Gilligan's theory (e.g. Unger and Crawford 1996) have argued that Gilligan's research (concerned with women making decisions about abortion) was **not comparable** with the rather more abstract dilemmas faced by Kohlberg's subjects.
- Gilligan was also accused of showing a **failure to explore other factors** than sex which could be related to differences in moral reasoning (e.g. social class, education, race/ethnicity).
- Gilligan also failed to explore the possibility that what **appeared** to be a sex difference in moral reasoning might also reflect women's **subordinate social position**, with perhaps the ethic of 'care and responsibility' being expressed by less powerful people generally, rather than just women.

Paragraph 4

● The alpha/beta bias distinction is just one way in which you might detect gender bias in psychological theories. Some theories are also **androcentric**, in that they only study men and yet apply the same findings to women. Again, you must think carefully about how you introduce this bias. It is important that you don't forget the critical commentary in this paragraph, as merely **identifying** an androcentric bias would be insufficient to capture the elusive AO2 marks. You can achieve your AO2 by considering the **consequence** of androcentrism as well as taking issue with an androcentric theory.

- Psychological theories such as Kohlberg's may also be seen as displaying an **androcentric bias** – one which offers an interpretation of women based on the lives of men.
- A consequence of androcentrism is that female development is often represented as a **departure from the norm of male development**, with the related inference that it is in some way 'abnormal' or 'pathological'.
- Freud's psychoanalytic theory explains how the young boy's identification with his father leads to the formation of a superego and of high moral standards. Girls, who do not experience the same Oedipal conflict, cannot, it appears, develop their superego to the same degree as boys.
- Feminist critics of Freudian psychoanalysis criticise its **culture-bound sexism**. Friedan (1965) condemns Freud's account of women on the grounds that he was a 'prisoner of his own culture' and therefore bound to write from that perspective.

Paragraph 5

● Not all psychologists see gender role as an **either/or** dichotomy. One that perhaps is biased towards a rather different view of gender role is Sandra Bem's concept of **androgyny**. In this next paragraph you can introduce Bem's main ideas but, as before, offer some critical commentary as you go along. Note that by introducing this rather different approach (i.e. an attempt by Bem to redress the gender-bias issues within psychology), you are showing evidence of **synopticity**.

- Bem (1975) presented the concept of **androgyny**, which represented a type of gender-role identity where the person scores highly on both masculine **and** feminine personality characteristics.
- Critics (e.g. Unger and Crawford 1996) have argued that **personality** variables such as androgyny do not correlate well with behaviour, with **situational** variables being far more important.
- Bem is critical of the way in which psychology **decontextualises** everything, and is even critical of her own individualism which is expressed in the concept of androgyny.
- Like many other writers in psychology, Bem advocates a removal of the whole idea of **gender polarisation** and the organisation of social life around these poles of **male** and **female**.

Paragraph 6

● As you stated at the beginning of this answer, you are not going to restrict yourself to just discussing **theories** that display a gender bias, but you will also look at the gender bias that is encountered in **research** in psychology. By introducing this variety of perspective in your answer you are also increasing the breadth of your commentary, and hence your **synoptic** content. You can introduce this part of the answer with Celia Kitzinger's contention that 'science is power' and then proceed to demonstrate how this view impacts on the **integrity** of scientific research.

■ Questions about sex similarities and differences are not just scientific questions, they are also highly **political** (Kitzinger 1997). Some of the answers to these questions have been used to **exclude** women from some occupations or to represent women as being **victims** of their own bodies.

■ The 'discovery' of **pre-menstrual syndrome**, during which female hormones become so unstable as to apparently render some women capable of murder, has led to an increase in experimental research in this area (Nicolson 1997).

■ Nicolson argues that many of the performance and mood differences traditionally identified between pre-menstrual women and others were products of **poor research design**. Several other well-designed studies, she claims, reporting no differences, were not published since their findings, being outside the existing paradigm, were subject to doubt.

Paragraph 7

● Okay, so this may be a luxury, but if time and motivation allow, why not include this little gem of information. According to some critics, bias may actually exist **within** feminist psychology, particularly when it comes to superimposing the issues of gender and ethnicity. This would make a good closing paragraph, and again gives you some valuable synoptic content.

■ Although psychologists are encouraged to develop a heightened awareness of human diversity in their writings and research investigations, this is not always in evidence.

■ Howitt and Owusu-Bempah (1994) argue that white feminist psychologists, although dealing effectively with the issues of women, have failed to adequately address the issues relating to **black** women.

■ In an analysis of American textbooks dealing with the psychology of women, Brown (1985) discovered that approximately one-third made almost **no** references at all to black women. One-third made only **brief** reference to black women, and one-third were **segregationist** – black women were represented only during references to the Third World.

■ Howitt suggests that rather than being sensitive to black experience, textbooks on the psychology of women **reproduce the non-feminist tradition** in psychology texts, but against black people rather than women.

ANNIE'S ANSWER TO QUESTION 2

Describe and evaluate arguments for and against the use of animals in psychological research. [30 marks]

Animals are used in psychological research for many reasons. One of these is that they give psychologists the chance to study things that might not be possible if they were to use human participants instead. This is a major scientific advantage in animal research, and because of this fact, it has been possible for researchers to bring about improvements in many areas of human life, most notably in the treatment of anxiety and other psychological disorders. These scientific advances have not been made easily though, as they are often achieved at considerable expense in terms of animal suffering. Some people believe that we should not carry out research on animals that we cannot also carry out on human beings. Otherwise we would be committing speciesism, by using one species for the advantage of another.

In order to justify the use of animals in psychological research, we should be confident that animals are sufficiently similar to human beings so that any comparisons are valid. Some psychologists (e.g. Green 1994) believe that there are sufficient similarities in the physiology and behaviour of all mammals for comparisons between different mammalian species to be valid. He argues that although the human brain is more highly developed than say a rat's brain, the basic physiology and functioning of the two are very similar. The behaviourists believed that humans and other mammals such as rats were so similar in terms of their evolutionary past that they developed a whole perspective on behaviour largely from the study of rats and pigeons. Critics of this view claim that humans and non-humans are not similar therefore any comparison between the behaviour of two unrelated species is worthless.

Another scientific argument in favour of animal research is the fact that scientists have developed some far less invasive procedures to study animals. These are known as the three Rs (replacement, reduction and refinement) and by using these procedures they are less likely to cause harm to animals. There are also strict laws governing the use of animals in research (such as the 1986 Use of Animals Act) and this means that scientists are forced to carry out their research in an ethically acceptable way. Britain has the tightest regulations about animal research anywhere in the world, so research is likely to be more ethically acceptable in the UK than anywhere else. Critics of this view claim that we should be trying harder to abolish animal research completely, and that if we were to consider the rights of animals then it would not matter how non-invasive the procedures were or how beneficial the research, they would still be unacceptable on ethical grounds.

This defence of animal research is not acceptable to all. Tom Regan believes that animals have rights not to be used as 'renewable resources' and have as many rights as human beings. One of these rights is the right to be treated with respect and not to be harmed regardless of the benefits to human beings. Regan also believes that animals have rights based on their 'inherent value' and we should not try to devalue them by treating them merely as research subjects. According to Regan and others, we have no right to treat animals differently to humans. Animal research is frequently assessed in terms of its potential costs and benefits, but if we calculate the benefits to human beings and the costs to animals then that is an example of speciesism. It is probably true that animal research has helped to lessen human suffering in many areas, but how has this helped the animals themselves?

Probably the most powerful argument against using animals in psychological research is that we simply have no right to do so. Animals cannot give their informed consent to take part in research, therefore what right have we to make them take part against their will? Although we can say we have the tightest regulations in the world for animal research, and scientists can reassure us that they are using procedures that minimise the suffering of animals, we are still causing them stress and pain just by experimenting on them. Even carrying out field experiments on animals in the wild can have lots of negative consequences for the animals concerned, so we should consider all the different ways in which we might harm animal subjects before using them in our research. In conclusion, the benefits of using animals are clear, but the fact that such benefits are achieved at great expense to the animals concerned means that we should begin to look for suitable alternatives instead of concentrating solely on animals.

(19/30)

This is a good paragraph and one that might either be used as an argument *against* animal research, or a *criticism* of the position outlined in the previous paragraph. Either way, it shows a good understanding of Regan's animal rights perspective.

There are a couple of new points made here (e.g. the problems of field experiments) but nothing much that hasn't already been addressed elsewhere in the essay. The same basic sentiments are being *repeated* (we gain knowledge at the expense of the animals themselves), although the wording is slightly different. Annie could have made something more out of the claim regarding *lack of informed consent*. It is precisely this fact that makes the need for tight regulation of animal research such a necessity.

Overall, an intelligent essay that does present *both* sides of the argument and shows a number of synoptic points as well. The *AO1* skills are better developed than the *AO2* skills, and this is the main reason why Annie has not done better. It is still good, but at 19/30 marks it is still only equivalent to a *Grade B*.

How to score full marks

Unpack the question carefully

- Although this question may simply look like 'the animal research' question, it is a reasonably complicated question in that it has several distinct parts to it. It would pay you to **spend a little time unpacking its requirements,** and then using the guidance in the previous section to carefully construct your response so that all these requirements are met. First of all you are required to include both arguments **for** animal research, and arguments **against**. Next you are required to both **describe** these arguments, and also to **evaluate** them. Finally, you are required to demonstrate your synoptic skills in both AO1 **and** AO2 domains. In other words, don't just charge in and deliver your best intentions without first giving due attention to **all** the different requirements of the question.

Make your intentions clear

- This is not an invitation to instruct the examiner what you intend to do, but rather a suggestion that you make it clear when you are using an argument as **evaluation** and when you are merely **describing** an argument. As the number of marks available for AO1 and AO2 is the same (15), **you** should be the person who decides what counts for what. If you intend material to be used evaluatively, use words like '**however**' or expressions such as '**in contrast to this position**' so that the examiner is clear how you intend this content to be marked. Remember, to get full marks in this essay you must go **beyond mere description** of the arguments; you must also **evaluate** them **effectively**.

Don't stand on a soapbox

- Questions such as this often bring out the best (and worst) from students. Many of you will have a healthy dislike of animal research in any form, and some of you may actually be committed anti-vivisectionists, vegans, or in some other way deplore the exploitation of animals. Now is not the time to vent your spleen. You should try (in fact the question requires it) to see both sides of the argument. Indeed, you are required to **evaluate** both sides of the argument. Your evaluation may be biased according to your standpoint on this issue, but just remember that it is **more important to do well in this exam than to impress an examiner** (who has probably heard it all before) with the strength of your feelings (of course you may disagree…).

Don't forget to be synoptic

- Although the need to be synoptic should not distract you from dealing with the prescriptions of the question, you should remember that the examiner is looking for evidence of your **synoptic skills** in this question. Annie has included a few different issues and made links with other perspectives and disciplines such as philosophy, physiology, psychopathology, evolutionary theory and comparative psychology. The answer would have been enhanced if she could have offered some **critical commentary** on these points. For example, animal research has been instrumental in developing better therapeutic approaches, but is there evidence that such research really **does** play such an important part in this field?

Question to try

Question 3

With reference to at least **two** areas of psychological investigation, discuss the ethics of socially sensitive research. [30 marks]

[Time allowed: 40 minutes]

Examiner's hints

● **The first thing to note about this question is that the synoptic element is spelled out for you**. You are asked to make reference to at least two areas of psychological investigation. These might be different branches of psychology (e.g. social and abnormal psychology) or different areas of study (such as 'understudied' relationships or cultural differences). There is also an opportunity to discuss a range of different ethical issues and their consequences, so synoptic opportunities abound in this question!

● **You should be careful to make sure that your content is really about socially sensitive research**, rather than simply including a range of ethical issues that are more general in their application. Ethical issues such as **deception** and **confidentiality** also apply to socially sensitive research, but you must discuss them in that context rather than leaving it to the examiner to make the relevant links on your behalf.

● Answering questions such as this can be extremely challenging in terms of all their constituent requirements. **Think for a moment about what is required**. First, you are required to show evidence of both **AO1** and **AO2** in your answer. This means that you are expected to raise some **relevant descriptive content** about the ethics of socially sensitive research and also **offer a critical commentary** on that content. Second, you are required to **demonstrate some synopticity in your answer** (in at least two different areas of investigation, remember) and then offer critical commentary on that. In practice it is easier than it sounds, as you will be interweaving all this information together and the examiner will award marks accordingly.

● Although this advice appears to suggest a 'throw it all in and someone else will make sense of it for you' approach, this is not the case. **It is up to you to monitor your answer at all times in order to ensure that you are providing what is really required in the answer**. Check the marking allocations at the beginning of this book, and put yourself in the place of the examiner. What mark would you give your answer? **Make it easy for the examiner to give you high marks by explicitly dealing with all the requirements of the question**.

Exam Questions

Time allowed: 40 minutes

Question 1

Discuss assumptions made about free will and/or determinism in **two or more** psychological theories. [30 marks]

Question 2

(a) Describe **two or more** examples of reductionism in psychological research.

[15 marks]

(b) Assess the contribution of reductionist explanations to our understanding of human behaviour. [15 marks]

Question 3

To what extent can it be claimed that Psychology is a science? [30 marks]

How to 'deconstruct' a question and plan an effective answer

This section deals with Question 1 above.

Mark allocation

- The word '**discuss**' is **an AO1** and **AO2** term requiring you to 'describe' (AO1) and 'evaluate' (AO2). In this question, as in all questions, there is an equal number of marks for each skill. **AO1** is knowledge and understanding and **AO2** is analysis and evaluation. If your answer fails to address **both** of these skills, or provides them in a very **unbalanced** way, you will simply lose the opportunity to pick up the marks available for that component. No matter how good the AO1 content, the maximum mark is still only 15 if no AO2 evaluation is present.

- In both AO1 and AO2 assessments of Unit 5 there are **synoptic criteria**. You will be assessed on your ability to include knowledge (AO1) and critical appreciation (AO2) of **different theoretical perspectives and/or methodological approaches** (see page 12 for a discussion of synopticity). Given the topic of this essay **it would be difficult *not* to be synoptic** as you will be discussing several theories (thus making links across the specification) and using different techniques to evaluate these theories. In addition, the very topic of your essay (free will/determinism) is synoptic as it is an overarching issue.

- You must respond **exactly** to the requirements of this question. It asks for **two or more** theories. If you include only one theory your essay will be marked on the '**partial performance criteria**' (a maximum of 9 marks AO1 and 9 marks AO2). If you cover more than two theories they will all receive credit, but the more theories you cover, the less detail you can hope to include in the 40 minutes allowed. One of the criteria for good AO1 marks is a balance between **depth** and **breadth**. This is called the '**depth–breadth trade-off**'.

🎯 Planning your response

- The first step in planning your response is to deconstruct the essay title. The key features are 'assumptions', 'free will and/or determinism' and 'two or more psychological theories'. This means that you must focus on '**assumptions**'. An assumption is something which is taken as being true without any proof. It is the basis of an approach or belief. This means that you are required to **examine** the assumptions made about determinism and/or free will in the particular theories that you discuss. You have the luxury of choosing to cover **free will and/or determinism**, a choice that will probably be influenced by your knowledge of theories that represent free will. Most candidates will know a reasonable amount about theories that represent determinist approaches and might restrict their knowledge of free will to be used for commentary/evaluation.

- The final consideration regards **how many** theories to cover. Given the depth/breadth trade-off, it might not be desirable to cover too many theories and therefore three theories might be a good compromise. This would provide increasing breadth but not too much to lose depth. Three theories would also provide more opportunities to display synopticity than just two theories.

- There are 40 minutes allowed for this question, so if you tackle three theories you could divide your answer into three 'chunks', each consisting of a paragraph of description and a paragraph of commentary. This gives a total of 6 paragraphs and just over 6 minutes of writing time for each (each paragraph about 150 words). The plan for every theory covered would be:

  - A description of the **assumptions** made about determinism (or free will) by the theory.
  - **Commentary** on this theory in relation to these assumptions (i.e. not a general evaluation of the theory), including reference to relevant issues/debates (**synoptic AO1**) as well as a commentary on them (**synoptic AO2**).

🎯 Synoptic signposts

- All essays on Unit 5 are assessed in terms of synopticity as well as the other criteria used in Unit 4. Synopticity and the synoptic criteria are discussed in the introduction of this book.

- These are some ideas about what synoptic material you might include when writing an essay on free will and determinism. AO1 material (description) is on the left and AO2 material (evaluation/commentary) is on the right.

Deterministic theories such as psychoanalysis assume that certain gender-related behaviours are inevitable.

Part of the reason that Freud's theory is so gender biased is that it was written at a time when there were large differences between the genders in terms of expectations.

The cultural setting you grow up in influences your beliefs, morals, attitudes and your own way of rearing your children.

If individuals are socialised within a particular type of culture (i.e. individualist or collectivist), that does not mean they will always have to behave in this way.

The use of deception removes the ability of research participants to **choose** whether to take part based on full knowledge of their role in the investigation.

Some psychologists, such as Milgram, have argued that deception is necessary in order to conduct some kinds of research which will provide important insights into human behaviour.

Paragraph 1

- You are not required to define determinism nor are marks gained for stating what you intend to do in this essay. You might as well plunge in straight away and show that you know exactly what is needed to answer this question. Don't forget that it is vital to 'score' synoptic points where relevant by mentioning other issues and debates, approaches and methodologies, and make links wherever possible across the specification.

  - **Behaviourist theory** is determinist.
  - The assumptions of **operant conditioning** are that any behaviour that is reinforced is more likely to be repeated whereas a behaviour that is punished will be less likely to be repeated. **Reinforcers and punishers determine later behaviour.**
  - The key assumption of **classical conditioning** is that **new associations** are learned when a reflex reaction is paired with a new stimulus. For example, if a bell is sounded every time a puff of air is blown in your eye, then you will 'learn' to blink when you hear a bell.
  - The basic assumption of these learning theories is that **all behaviour is determined by forces outside of our free will**.

Paragraph 2

- In this next paragraph it is important to offer commentary/evaluation that is pertinent to this question, i.e. related to the determinist nature of behaviourism rather than a critique of behaviourism in general. One way to display synopticity is through references to behaviourist theories from across the specification.

  - The determinist nature of behaviourism has advantages. It has formed the basis of many successful theories. Skinner used operant conditioning to explain **language acquisition**. It has also been used to explain **attachment** and the **development of mental illnesses**.
  - Classical conditioning has also been used to explain mental disorders such as **phobias**. Such explanations have led to **successful applications** as in the treatment of mental disorders using behavioural techniques.
  - There are, however, many alternative accounts for these behaviours which raise doubts about the **validity** of learning theory. For example, Chomsky proposed that language acquisition is related to **innate processes**. Similarly Seligman suggested that phobias can be explained in terms of **innate preparedness**.
  - However, both these biological alternatives are just as determinist as the behaviourist approach. A completely contrasting approach, and one based on free will, is humanistic psychology. Humanistic psychologists would describe mental disorders more in terms of **subjective experience** and emphasise the importance of **self-determination** (free will) in therapy.

Paragraph 3

- Now you need to select a second theory and again take as your starting point the assumptions of the theory. This paragraph will score on synopticity by (a) making a new link across the specification and (b) considering various different **aspects** of Freud's theory.

  - A second theory which is highly determinist is Freud's account of **personality development**. Freud assumed that the infant is born with certain drives. These drives interact with the environment in such a way that the infant's needs are either satisfied or not.
  - According to Freud, the outcome is **predictable** (i.e. determined). An infant whose oral needs are not satisfied at that stage will go on to become an oral aggressive personality – aggressive and dominating.
  - Freud also predicted other behaviours. He suggested that the individual copes with anxiety by using **ego defences** which **repress** anxious thoughts. Such anxieties remain in the

unconscious mind and are then expressed in other ways. Because we have no control over them, these repressed thoughts motivate our behaviour in a determinist way.

◎ Paragraph 4

- It is important to consider what **synoptic material** might be introduced in this paragraph. Reference to other theories (links across the specification) with commentary (AO2) on these theories is one possibility. Appropriate content might include:

  ■ Freud's theory of personality has had an enormous **influence** both inside psychology and elsewhere.

  ■ Freud made contributions to our understanding of **gender and moral development** as well as his largest contribution, which was to our understanding of **mental disorders**. For example, he argued that **depression** often occurs as a reaction to the loss of an important relationship. An individual who identifies with the lost person experiences anger, and this is repressed and then directed inwards towards the self. Experiences of loss later in life cause the individual to re-experience childhood episodes.

  ■ Other theories of personality can be contrasted with Freud's approach but most of them are also quite determinist, such as **learning theory** or **biological/genetic** accounts. Bandura, in a social learning account, introduced the notion of **reciprocal determinism** where it is proposed that each individual selects what behaviours to imitate, based on their personality, beliefs, and cognitive abilities. This introduces an element of free will into personality development.

  ■ One difficulty with the determinist view of personality development is that it conflicts with the belief that adults have **responsibility** for their own actions. If an individual commits a crime it would not be permissible to argue in court that criminal behaviours were not under the individual's control. The law essentially upholds the principle that each individual has free will and personal responsibility. These are **ethical** issues which are difficult to fully resolve. For example, in the case of young children who commit murders, can we hold them responsible for what they have done?

◎ Paragraph 5

- You must resist the temptation to begin discussing determinism more widely. Such material would be creditworthy but it is not the backbone of this essay, which requires a focus on **assumptions in theories**. A possible third theory would be:

  ■ The theory of **evolution** is another highly determinist account, the central assumption being that any behaviour that continues to exist must be adaptive. Such behaviours are inherited and **predispose** (i.e. determine) us to act in ways that promote survival and reproduction.

  ■ There are many examples of this throughout psychology, such as **sociobiological** explanations of **altruism** and **relationships**.

◎ Paragraph 6

- The next step is to offer commentary on this third theory. Some possible issues might be:

  ■ Like all determinist explanations, evolutionary theory appears to suggest that certain behaviours are unavoidable. This may be **unacceptable**, as in the case of Thornhill's attempt to justify rape on evolutionary grounds. Thornhill and Thornhill (1983) argued that men who are unable to mate are driven to select an alternative strategy. Some people object to such arguments, arguing that humans have the capacity for free will.

- It may be possible to understand the apparent determinism/free will contradiction in terms of **James's** concept of **soft determinism**. James (1890) suggested that there is a distinction between behaviour that is highly constrained by the situation (and appears involuntary, i.e. determined) and behaviour that is only modestly constrained by the situation (and appears voluntary). Behaviour is determined in both cases, however in the latter situation it seems 'freer'. In this way we might argue that, while our genes direct behaviour in some situations, we do not always have to be constrained by them.

◎ Paragraph 7

- A final paragraph is needed as a conclusion. **It is important that such a conclusion does not repeat information already offered but is a genuine attempt to state some kind of final opinion** – an opinion informed by psychology.

  - The solution may lie in something like James's determinism, or Heather's (1976) view that much of behaviour is predictable but not inevitable, individuals are free to choose their behaviour but this is usually from within a fairly limited repertoire.

SARITA'S ANSWER TO QUESTION 2

(a) Describe **two or more** examples of reductionism in psychological research. [15 marks]

One example of a reductionist explanation in psychology is the theory of dreams proposed by McCarley and Hobson (1977). They suggested that dreams are what we experience when asleep because random activation is interpreted as if it was produced by real movements or sensations. When you are asleep there is a block on these nervous signals so the brain misinterprets random signals. This account reduces the rich, subjective experience of dreams to nervous impulses that have been misread.

In contrast Freud's account of dreaming is much more complex but nevertheless could also be described as reductionist because he suggested that dreams are symbolic. The manifest (actual) content of the dream represents the latent (true) meaning. This representation is achieved through symbols which make something that is threatening appear less threatening. This account suggests that the content of our dream can be explained through (reduced to) a set of symbols. Freud's theories tend to reduce human behaviour to a simpler set of processes.

Neurological accounts of behaviour, such as Hobson and McCarley's, are generally reductionist as are physiological accounts because they reduce behaviour to a set of simpler processes in the body. Schachter and Singer's theory of emotion is an example of this. This theory proposes that the emotion we experience occurs as a result of physiological arousal which is then labelled on the basis of expectations. This account suggests that the experience of emotion is largely based on arousal, i.e. it reduces emotion to an arousal state.

Biological accounts of behaviour include genetics as well as physiology, and genetic explanations are also reductionist. Sociobiological explanations of altruism or the formation of relationships reduce these behaviours to the principles of natural selection. The basic argument is that individuals possess certain behaviours because the behaviours are adaptive. An individual with the genes for these behaviours is more likely to survive and reproduce. This means that, potentially, we can explain all behaviour in terms of adaptiveness and the genetic blueprint for each individual.

Sarita began the first paragraph with what sounds like an evaluation of Hobson and McCarley's account of dreaming. *Such evaluation would attract no credit in part (a) and might be exported to part (b) if it would be relevant there.* However, Sarita has used Freud's theory in the second paragraph to show how seemingly unreductionist theories may also be reductionist – in a different way.

Sarita has taken the breadth rather than the depth route to answering part (a). She has constructed a very fluent account covering a variety of different examples and, for each, offered a reasonable amount of detail. *The breadth of examples offered increases the AO1 synoptic element of this essay.*

The behaviourist approach, which is usually contrasted with the biological approach (one is nurture the other is nature), is also reductionist. Behaviourists reduce behaviour to stimulus-response links. An organism is born as a blank slate and gradually builds up more and more complex behaviours through association (classical conditioning) and reinforcement (operant conditioning). The new behaviours represent new links learned between a stimulus and a response.

(b) Assess the contribution of reductionist explanations to our understanding of human behaviour. [15 marks]

There is no requirement in the second part of this question to assess the examples offered in part (a). The assessment can be of *any examples*, though it is important to avoid giving any further descriptions which are relevant only to part (a). *A well-organised answer will place all descriptions in part (a) and assessment in part (b).*

Some people are very critical of the reductionist approach, saying that it oversimplifies complex problems. In the case, for example, of neurophysiological explanations of dreaming the reductionist explanation tries to make out that dreaming is a very simple process. This may mislead psychologists into accepting this explanation and prevent them researching further and finding out about other possibilities. The end result of this is that we may only end up with rather incomplete explanations of behaviour.

A further criticism that is made of reductionist explanations is that they may not be appropriate. If we want to explain the experience of emotion it is not appropriate to seek a physiological explanation because this only offers an explanation at this level. It does not address what Rose (1976) has referred to as 'different levels of explanation'. The wholly reductionist approach overlooks more mentalistic and social explanations.

Sarita has approached this part of the question by examining, first of all, the arguments against the reductionist approach. She has made reference to some of the examples provided in part (a) as a useful way to *elaborate* her points.

On the other hand there are reasons in favour of the reductionist approach. First of all, those psychologists who prefer an empirical, scientific approach need to reduce the behaviour they are studying to operationalised variables and in doing so they are reducing behaviour. There are many examples of this in memory experiments as well as experiments on social behaviour. Some people criticise this approach for producing meaningless data about human behaviour but such experiments (e.g. those on eyewitness testimony) have produced useful findings that have been applied in real life.

A further plus for the reductionist approach is that it is an important part of understanding anything. Such explanations may not be the whole explanation of any behaviour but they may be useful. For example, when we want to understand mental illness it may be that hormones and genes are part of the story but there are probably a host of other factors (the diathesis–stress model). But the biological explanation leads to biological treatments, such as using drugs, and these treatments are successful. This supports the usefulness of the reductionist approach.

In conclusion it may be fair to say that reductionist explanations are necessary but not always sufficient.

(21/30)

There is no requirement to write a concluding statement, as Sarita has here. In this case it is *insufficiently elaborated* to be worth much. The rest of part (b) is *reasonably informed* and the material has been *effectively* used.

Overall, this is a competent essay which hasn't achieved 'substantial evidence of breadth and depth' (AO1) but is reasonably informed and coherent (AO2), giving a mark of 21/30, probably a Grade A.

How to score full marks

Keep your eye on the ball

● It is important, when writing essays on Unit 5, that you provide **evidence of synopticity** as well as the specific content for the essay. However, there is always the danger that you might go overboard and end up trying to be too synoptic and losing marks because **there is no content!** You must remember to focus on the main topic of the essay while always bearing in mind that, in this unit exam, you must display **all you have learned** over the whole course (i.e. demonstrate synopticity).

Exporting and importing in parted questions

● Examiners use the following rule when marking parted questions: 'If a candidate includes material that is **clearly relevant** and would earn marks in one part of a question, it should remain (when determining marks) **regardless** of whether it might earn more marks elsewhere. If the material is only **peripherally relevant** or **irrelevant** to one part of the question and would earn marks in the other part, then it should be "**exported**" (when determining marks) to that part.' In this instance, Sarita might have included some evaluation in part (a), where it would receive no credit. The examiner would then **export** that material to part (b) and give it credit there.

Be fair

● When you are asked to assess something, you may be required to examine both **strengths and limitations**. In such cases you will only get partial marks if you cover only strengths or only limitations. In Sarita's answer there was no requirement to give strengths **and** limitations, but a good answer would demonstrate a balanced view, as Sarita has.

Question 3

To what extent can it be claimed that Psychology is a science?   [30 marks]

[Time allowed: 40 minutes]

Examiner's hints

● A very general essay title like this may appear to be a gift but you must take care **not** to write everything you know but to present a **well-balanced answer** to the question which addresses both the **depth and breadth criteria**, and is **well-structured**. In terms of balance you should clearly consider the extent to which Psychology can be claimed to be a science and the extent to which this claim is not valid.

● Before attempting to engage in such a discussion it is important to be clear about what we mean by 'science'. It is often the case, when writing examination essays in Psychology, that definitions are not required and would attract very few marks. However, in this case, a **core part of the debate is a consideration of what we do mean by science**. Only then are we in a position to judge whether Psychology is or is not a science. It is not just experiments that are scientific; qualitative methods such as discourse analysis aim to be objective as well. But are they scientific?

● Beyond the question of whether Psychology can be considered to be a science is the issue of whether all psychologists regard science as the holy grail. There are **other ways of collecting knowledge** about behaviours and these methods may be **equally valid**.

● In your response you must always bear the **synopticity criteria** in mind. The more you can make references to different topic areas across psychology, as examples of the points you are making, the more **credit** you will be given for demonstrating an awareness of different theoretical perspectives and/or methodological approaches. Don't forget that there is credit both for a description (AO1) of such perspectives/approaches and a critical appreciation (AO2) of them.

The *Approaches* questions are quite different from all other questions on your A2 paper. You will be required to apply your knowledge and understanding of any **two** approaches to a novel situation or psychological phenomenon presented in stimulus material given in the examination questions. These approaches might be selected from:

(a) biological/medical, behavioural, psychodynamic and cognitive (as specified in AS/A2 Individual Differences);

(b) others which appear in the specification, but which are not compulsory (i.e. they are not specified in AS or are specified in a non-compulsory section of A2), such as social constructionism, humanistic and evolutionary psychology;

(c) those deriving from other, related disciplines, such as sociology, biology and philosophy (for example, symbolic interactionism and functionalism).

Exam Questions

Question 1

When Julie was at university, she was very carefree and, some would say, rather frivolous. After graduation she started a career and moved out of the home she had shared with her parents for the last twenty-one years. She soon began to realise that being an adult was not that easy, and with that was the realisation that adulthood also meant that she must now be a responsible contributor to society. Living in a flat on her own was lonely, and she telephoned her mother a great deal. She also found solace in her cuddly toys, and spent much of her time talking to them, and treating them as if they were children. When visitors came she would insist that at least one of her favourite toys sat with them, and would get very angry if visitors ever made fun of her toys or mistreated them.

Key concept: Julie's need for cuddly toys.

(a) Describe how **two** approaches might try to explain Julie's need for cuddly toys.
[6 + 6 marks]

(b) Assess **one** of these explanations of Julie's need for cuddly toys in terms of its strengths and limitations. [6 marks]

(c) Analyse how **one** of these approaches might investigate Julie's need for cuddly toys. [6 marks]

(d) Evaluate the use of this method of investigation of Julie's need for cuddly toys. [6 marks]

Question 2

Matt is a bright if apparently lazy 18-year-old. He gets up late most days and spends most of his waking hours glued to his computer playing games. These tend to be advanced 'strategy games' frequently involving multiple players via the Internet. His parents despair of this behaviour and frequently criticise him for not spending more time engaged in 'healthy' outdoor pursuits or looking for a job.

Key concept: Matt's involvement with computer games.

(a) Describe how **two** approaches might try to explain Matt's involvement with computer games. [6 + 6 marks]

(b) Assess **one** of these explanations of Matt's involvement with computer games in terms of its strengths and limitations. [6 marks]

(c) Analyse how **one** of these approaches might investigate Matt's involvement with computer games. [6 marks]

(d) Evaluate the use of this method of investigation of Matt's involvement with computer games. [6 marks]

CASSIE'S ANSWER TO QUESTION 1

(a) Describe how **two** approaches might try to explain Julie's need for cuddly toys.

[6 + 6 marks]

One explanation could be the evolutionary explanation. Babies have certain features (such as big eyes and squashed nose) that make them irresistible to us. Film-makers like Walt Disney have made a fortune out of exploiting these features with characters like Bambi. The same thing applies to cuddly toys. Many of these are given baby-type features, and we are inclined towards wanting to look after them. Julie may well feel very protective towards her cuddly toys because they are like babies to her and she is programmed to want to look after them. Some evolutionary theorists even believe that we are programmed to look after all babies because they must be disease resistant and therefore would make good mates for our own offspring. This would explain why Julie has so many toys and why she feels so protective to them all.

(6/6)

A second explanation could be the psychoanalytic explanation. This explanation suggests that we develop through a series of stages and have to deal with lots of different problems within these stages. For example, we have to be toilet trained when we are about 18 months. It is possible that Julie's feelings towards her toys signal a reluctance to become a proper 'adult' by clinging to what is left of her childhood. If she has recently left home and is living on her own, she may feel under a lot of strain and this is one way of her staying 'child-like'. She also rings her mother a great deal, so that also suggests she is reluctant to strike out on her own.

(4/6)

This is an *excellent* first explanation. Rather than just offering an outline of evolutionary explanations of behaviour in general, Cassie has offered a *clear* and *informed* account of this explanation. There is an impressive explanatory point made in this final sentence.

The first part of this explanation is a *little too general* (e.g. the reference to toilet training), but the second part is much more *focused*. The concept of *regression* might have been introduced appropriately here.

(b) Assess **one** of these explanations of Julie's need for cuddly toys in terms of its strengths and limitations. [6 marks]

The strengths of an evolutionary explanation for Julie's need for cuddly toys are that it does help to explain why such a behaviour was adaptive in the first place. Perhaps it was very important for mothers to stay close to their children because it was such a hostile environment. Another strength is that it explains why people the world over have the same need for cuddly toys.

The limitations of this explanation include the fact that we have no actual physical evidence to support this explanation — it is all just speculation. It is also inappropriate to assume that another explanation (e.g. a cognitive one) is not responsible for Julie's preference for cuddly toys over other types of contact (e.g. with people). She may well have been let down in a relationship and decided that the only things she can 'trust' not to let her down are her cuddly toys that have 'stuck with her' from childhood.

5/6

(c) Analyse how **one** of these approaches might investigate Julie's need for cuddly toys. [6 marks]

An evolutionary explanation cannot be tested in a laboratory but there are a number of ways that evolutionary psychologists might investigate the basis of Julie's need for cuddly toys. They might, for example, carry out twin studies to see if this behaviour runs in Julie's family. If it did it would suggest that the need for cuddly toys had a genetic basis rather than being learned.

2/6

(d) Evaluate the use of this method of investigation of Julie's need for cuddly toys. [6 marks]

Twin studies cannot tell us much about the origins of a behaviour such as this as twins may not be representative of the population as a whole. For example, members of Julie's family may have experienced the same sort of upbringing so would behave in the same way. It is also possible that the investigators would know the people they were studying were related so they would be looking for similarities rather than differences.

3/6

20/30

How to score full marks

Select the right sort of approach

- When you select your two approaches to answer this question, **make sure you can sustain one of these throughout all the questions that follow**. Cassie might have done better to have chosen her second alternative for question parts (b) to (d). It is probably easier to criticise psychoanalytic explanations and methods of investigation than it is to do the same thing for evolutionary explanations **unless** you are thoroughly prepared.

Make sure you apply your approach to the topic in question

- In every area of psychology, psychologists use different 'approaches' to explain behaviour. The intention of the *Approaches* question is to assess your understanding of the approaches (perspectives) that psychologists use when explaining behaviour. For example, when you studied attachment you probably considered Bowlby's theory (a psychodynamic, evolutionary approach) and perhaps the learning theory (behavioural) approach. In this question you are given a novel situation and asked to **apply your understanding** of an approach to this situation. You are **not** being asked to simply explain the approach, but the application of that approach to the issue given. Cassie has coped well with this demand, but occasionally wanders off into a less effective general discussion of the approach itself.

Strengths and limitations

- In part (b) of these *Approaches* questions you will be asked to assess the **strengths and limitations** of one of your chosen explanations. You will lose marks if you don't include both strengths **and** limitations (a maximum of 4/6 marks for strengths or limitations only). Remember also that these strengths and limitations need to be **related to the issue at hand**, not general strengths and limitations of a particular psychological approach.

You can't predict but you can prepare

- The *Approaches* question differs from the other questions on Unit 5 and all those on Unit 4. It is not an 'essay' question. You are not required to display your knowledge and critical understanding of a material covered in specific topic areas. You may even feel that you can't do any revision for this question. However, given the predictability of the questions, you could at least **prepare some notes** on how the major approaches (such as behaviourism, social psychology, evolutionary theory etc.) tend to explain behaviour, the strengths and limitations of these explanations, their investigative methods and associated evaluation. This is not the same as having a prepared answer, it is simply a case of having the **right tools at hand** to do the job. Just remember, if Claude Monet went out intending to paint a winter scene, he probably took with him a fair amount of white paint!

Question to try

Question 2

Matt is a bright if apparently lazy 18 year-old. He gets up late most days and spends most of his waking hours glued to his computer playing games. These tend to be advanced 'strategy games' frequently involving multiple players via the Internet. His parents despair of this behaviour and frequently criticise him for not spending more time engaged in 'healthy' outdoor pursuits or looking for a job.

Key concept: Matt's involvement with computer games.

(a) Describe how **two** approaches might try to explain Matt's involvement with computer games.   [6 + 6 marks]

(b) Assess **one** of these explanations of Matt's involvement with computer games in terms of its strengths and limitations.   [6 marks]

(c) Analyse how **one** of these approaches might investigate Matt's involvement with computer games.   [6 marks]

(d) Evaluate the use of this method of investigation of Matt's involvement with computer games.   [6 marks]

Examiner's hints

- When selecting a question in the examination itself, you should look (and think) **carefully** about **both** questions, and mentally rehearse how you might deal with **all** the demands of both questions. This question deals with a situation that many of us find familiar, but can you really offer an intelligible explanation of it with the resources that you have available? The alternative question may look less interesting but is easier to answer. It's your call.

- Although most people will stick to the same approach through parts (b) to (d), the question does allow you to choose a **different approach** for parts (c) and (d) from the one you chose for part (b). It should, however, be one of the approaches that you described in part (a) rather than a totally new approach.

- The first part of this question is **AO1** and the next three parts **AO2**. This may appear a little strange, particularly as in the third part of the question you are **describing** how you might investigate this problem from within a chosen psychological approach. However, being able to look at the different components of your chosen approach and decide how these might be marshalled into an effective investigation of Matt's behaviour actually constitutes the skill of **analysis**.

- **Keep an eye on the clock when answering this question**. It is easy to get carried away answering one part of the question. For example, when addressing the requirements of part (c), you might drift into an inappropriately detailed account of all the different aspects of the investigation that takes up far more than the 6 minutes or so available. It obviously takes practice to present effective answers within clearly defined time limits, but it is necessary to make sure that you pick up sufficient marks in the other parts of the question.

- Make sure you stay **focused** on the issue at all times. Remember you are trying to demonstrate your ability to **apply** a particular approach to a novel situation, you are **not** simply demonstrating your knowledge of an approach and its investigative methods.

Answers to Questions to try

How to score full marks

(a) Batson's empathy-altruism hypothesis (Batson 1991) explains altruistic behaviour as a consequence of empathetic concern for another person who needs help. According to this model we experience empathy if we feel an emotional response that is consistent with another person's emotional state (e.g. feeling sad when they are sad). Batson believed that as a result of experiencing empathetic concern for another person, we are therefore motivated to help them when they are in distress. Empathy consists of a number of different components, including the ability to see things from another person's perspective, the experience of personal distress, and finally empathetic concern for the other person. Batson believed that seeing things from the perspective of the other person was crucial in the development of empathetic concern. If the perspective of the other person is not taken, we are more likely to experience personal distress without the empathetic concern that leads to helping.

> **Examiner's comment**
> This is a good opening paragraph, **concise** and **full of information**, which sets out the main points of Batson's empathy-altruism model. There is no attempt to wander off the required task by including needless evaluation, and **examples are not overused**, as is often the case in answers to questions such as this. An excellent opening, and a good example of an **effective précis**.

Cialdini's negative-state relief model (Cialdini et al. 1987) claims that when we come across a person in distress, it creates a negative emotional state in us (such as sadness or guilt). As this state is unpleasant, we are motivated to get rid of it in whatever way we can. People tend to learn during childhood that helping others in need is a positive behaviour that will make them feel good about themselves. Helping someone in need, therefore, is personally rewarding, and we are able to eliminate our negative state. According to the negative-state relief model, the main objective in helping behaviour is actually the enhancement of our own mood, with such behaviour being egoistic rather than altruistic. Cialdini believed that it didn't matter whether the negative emotions were already present before the opportunity to help arose, or were aroused by the situation itself. In either situation, helping someone in need is seen as a powerful antidote to any negative feelings we may be experiencing.

> **Examiner's comment**
> As with the first paragraph, this second one also presents a **concise and effective summary** of an acceptable explanation of altruism. Note that although this theory explains helping behaviour as being **egoistic** (i.e. self-serving), this is still an explanation of what **appears** to be altruistic behaviour. This is also evidence of sound and effective **time management** with each of these opening two paragraphs being around 150–160 words (and therefore making good use of the 7.5 minutes available for each 'component' of this question).

(b) It is a widely held belief that individualist societies (such as the US and UK) stress the need for individual achievement (i.e. *independence*), whilst collectivist societies (such as China and Russia) stress *interdependence* where individuals depend on each other. Therefore, differences in the altruistic behaviour of individuals may be interpreted in terms of the dominant cultural characteristics of their society. Nadler (1986) compared Israeli city dwellers with those living on a kibbutz in terms of whether they would be willing to seek and receive help from others. In support of the individualist/collectivist distinction, Nadler found that those who had been raised communally were more likely to help than those raised in a city, especially when the help was seen to benefit the group rather than just the individual. Although research has found evidence for such cultural differences in altruistic behaviour, this does not mean that all members of a particular culture would behave in the same way. All cultures have wide variations in the behaviour of their members, and other cultural rules (e.g. the need to help only family and close friends) often override the need to act altruistically to all.

> **Examiner's comment**
> This paragraph does not fall into the trap of merely describing cultural differences in altruistic behaviour, it **uses** the Nadler study to demonstrate that research evidence does in fact **support** the commonly held assumptions about individualist and collectivist cultures. It also includes a cautionary note that not all members of a culture would act the same and that **intracultural** differences may be every bit as significant as **intercultural** differences.

One problem for any assessment of cultural differences in altruistic behaviour arises from the context in which altruistic behaviour has been studied. Laboratory studies (the chosen method of enquiry for many Western social psychologists including Batson and Cialdini) have tended to show that people will often go out of their way to *avoid* seeking help from others. However, field studies (particularly those involving participants from Asian cultures) have tended to show that people *will* seek help when in need. This contrast in findings may not be the product of cultural differences alone. Laboratory-based studies tend to lack the social context of help seeking. Laboratory participants encounter anonymous fellow participants over a limited time period. As a result, there would seem little point in trying to develop a social relationship in such a context. In the real world, however, people actively seek out the help of others to *extend* their social relationships (Moghaddam 1998).

> **Examiner's comment**
> This is a **very perceptive point** that challenges the **validity** of the methods used to study altruistic behaviour in different cultures, and suggests that at least part of the differences we find may be explained in terms of the **context** of the study. This is particularly effective because it contributes handsomely to the requirement to **assess** the extent of cultural differences. The extent, we might conclude, is not as extensive as psychological research has claimed. This is a **well-planned and executed response** to what is, potentially, a quite difficult question. It would receive the **full 12 marks** available for each part of the question, and is typical of an excellent **Grade A** answer.

2 Physiological Psychology

How to score full marks

Studies in the early part of the twentieth century found that extreme emotions such as aggression were controlled by brain structures. Research showed that stimulation of areas such as the hypothalamus and thalamus could produce threat and attack behaviour in cats. Also, surgically removing the cerebral cortex could lead to 'decorticate rage' where the animal would show an extreme aggressive response to even the slightest stimulus. This showed that aggressive behaviour was organised by brain structures outside the cortex, but it was cortical structures that determined whether or not aggressive behaviour was exhibited. A number of studies have suggested that the right hemisphere of the cerebral cortex is more important than the left for some aspects of emotion. Adolphs et al. (1996) found that brain-damaged people who had damage in their right hemisphere often had difficulty recognising other people's emotions from their facial expressions.

MacLean (1939) established that the limbic system played a particularly important role in emotional behaviours. He discovered that the relative size of the limbic system varies little across different mammalian species, and is responsible for controlling many of the primitive emotions that all mammals have in common. Research has also shown that stimulation of a part of the limbic system known as the amygdala can lead to aggressive behaviour. MacLean (1954) found that people whose epilepsy originated in the amygdala often experienced aggressive impulses before, during or just after an epileptic attack. Lentz et al. (1982) also demonstrated that the brain disease 'rabies' which attacks a number of brain areas, including the amygdala, produces extreme aggressive behaviour in rabid animals. Removal of other brain structures can lead to extreme placidity. Damage to the temporal lobe, for example, can lead to the Klüver-Bucy syndrome. Klüver and Bucy found that monkeys that were previously wild and aggressive would not exhibit normal fears after temporal lobe damage.

Although research has highlighted the importance of the amygdala in the production of emotional responses to stimuli, it cannot decide for itself whether to display an emotional reaction. It appears that several other neural mechanisms are responsible for activating the amygdala when detecting a threatening stimulus. Some emotional reactions involving simple stimuli may be initiated by the thalamus. This claim is supported by studies that have found that lesions in this area disrupt the learning of a conditioned emotional response to a simple auditory stimulus. For more complex stimuli, however, other areas of the brain must be involved. Perceiving a social situation as threatening, for example, is obviously far more complex than perceiving the emotional threat in a single stimulus. Research has suggested that the orbitofrontal cortex plays a special role in this respect, and it was this belief that appeared to have justified the development of the prefrontal lobotomy for the relief of negative emotional experiences.

Most of the early research has been carried out on non-human animals. Green (2000) suggests that such studies are restricted to emotional behaviour, and can therefore tell us little about the way in which animals were feeling. The use of animals has also restricted the range of emotions that can be studied. Most studies have concentrated on extreme emotions such as fear and aggression, rather than the more subtle emotions that characterise human experience. Despite the similarities between the human brain and other mammalian brains, the human brain, particularly the cerebral cortex, is undoubtedly more complex than non-human brains. It is, therefore, inappropriate to extrapolate too much from non-humans to humans in this area. Later studies that have used humans as research subjects have largely overcome this problem, but most of these have concentrated on people with brain damage (e.g. Adolphs et al. 1996). Therefore it has been difficult to disentangle the effect of the brain damage itself from other related experiences that may have a determining effect on the emotion being studied.

> **Examiner's comment**
> A very good **critical** paragraph where the material is specifically relevant to that previously described. It draws in previous material (e.g. the Adolphs et al. reference) to provide a context for its criticisms, and the reference to the inappropriateness of animal studies is qualified in a highly efficient way. This **effective** use of critical material is what sets very good AO2 apart from the more run-of-the-mill responses. Overall, this is a very **well-informed and carefully constructed response** to the question.

3 Cognitive Psychology

How to score full marks

Divided attention describes the ability to allocate attention to two or more tasks at the same time. One explanation is the central capacity model proposed by Kahneman (1973). According to this model there is a central processor that allocates one central pool of attention. The amount of capacity that is available at any one time varies depending on circumstances. When you are wide awake you have increased capacity. If you are engaged in several tasks at once this reduces central capacity. Motivation can increase capacity. When tasks are more automatic this reduces the capacity needed for a task. Essentially there are two key assumptions: first, that there is some central capacity (attention or effort) which has limited resources, and second, that the ability to perform two tasks together depends on the demands placed on those resources by the two tasks.

> **Examiner's comment**
> This first paragraph is **packed full of detail**. It starts **straight into the answer**, earning marks immediately rather than wasting time with an elegant but uncreditworthy preamble. The concept of capacity is **well explained with lots of examples** of how capacity is increased and decreased, ending with a **summary** of the key assumptions.

A study by Bourke et al. (1996) supported this model. They gave participants two simultaneous tasks and found that the random letter generation task caused greatest difficulty in terms of interference (slowing down) other tasks. This was presumably because such a task placed the *greatest* demand on central capacity. The tone identification task interfered least, again presumably because of the load on the central capacity (this time a lower demand). They also found that when two tasks were very different this did not reduce performance.

This central capacity model has certain strengths, namely that it can explain both focused and divided attention and can account for the effects of task difficulty (in Bourke's study) and of practice. The effects of practice were shown in a study by Spelke et al. (1976), who trained two participants to perform two quite complex tasks simultaneously (read for comprehension and take down dictation). Eventually they could be performed easily in parallel.

However, the concept of 'central capacity' is rather vague; Allport (1980) pointed out that there is no independent definition of it. Another problem, raised by Revelle (1993), is that the model can't explain the Yerkes-Dodson law which states that too much arousal reduces performance. This model would predict that arousal goes on increasing capacity. Furthermore the model can't explain some effects of task similarity. For example in another study, Segal and Fusella (1970) showed that some similar tasks caused more interference than others which would not be predicted by the theory.

> **Examiner's comment**
> There's no law that says a 'chunk' of the essay has to be a whole paragraph. The second 'chunk' of this essay, evaluating the first explanation, considers various means of evaluation. Research studies have been used both to **support** and **challenge** the model, and description of these is kept **minimal** in order to score AO2 credit. This evaluation is **coherently elaborated and well informed.**

An alternative theory is Allport's (1989) modular theory. This theory proposes that the brain has various specific processing mechanisms termed 'modules'. Each module has a set capacity and each module is independent of the others. This fits well with neurophysiological evidence about areas of the brain that are dedicated to certain tasks. For example, Wernicke's area is associated with speech comprehension based on evidence from brain damage. Maguire et al.'s (1997) study of taxi drivers showed that the right hippocampus was active when they were recalling routes around London but not information about landmarks, indicating a special location for procedural memory.

> **Examiner's comment**
> The second model is briefly described and examples from neurophysiology used both as **further explanation** and **supporting evidence**, gaining credit for both AO1 and AO2. **You are not required to give both explanations in the same amount of detail in order to obtain full marks.**

This model has the advantage of being able to account for task similarity because when one is trying to do two things that are similar they will both be competing for activity in the same module. We can cope when tasks are different because they use different, independent modules. So this model accounts for task interference on similar tasks and lack of interference on different tasks. The model can also explain automated tasks which use the same module because, through automation, the task uses less of the resource available in the module.

However, it is difficult to disprove the model. The model can explain virtually any finding by suggesting that there is simply another module. This makes it possible to fit the model to any set of new facts.

> **Examiner's comment**
> The second explanation has been evaluated **coherently** and again demonstrates that the candidate is **well informed.**

Such theories have important practical applications because many accidents are the result of problems during dual-task performance. Thus, one would hope that such theoretical models can provide us with ideas about how to reduce these accidents. For example by reducing the number of tasks, or making it so that an individual does not have to deal with too many similar tasks at once.

> **Examiner's comment**
> The essay ends with some commentary on the **practical value** of this research. Again the point is not just stated but **further amplification is offered** to demonstrate the candidate's understanding. Overall, the essay is **well structured,** giving a sense of **competence** and **clarity.**

🎯 How to score full marks

The idea of 'cognitive changes' covers many different aspects of an older person's behaviour, including the intelligence of older people and their memory and mental reaction times. Physically there are obvious changes. Older people get smaller, slower, weaker, and fewer in number. But do their cognitive (mental) abilities actually decline?

> **Examiner's comment**
> This is an **effective introductory paragraph** which may get no direct marks but does provide a useful **framework** for the essay. **Commentary** is also **embedded** in it because the candidate notes that there are obvious physical changes but asks whether it follows that there are also cognitive changes.

Wechsler (1955) used data from his IQ test and reported that, according to this test, IQ peaks around the age of 30 and declines thereafter. Other research has found that such declines may be related to particular aspects of intelligence. For example, Schultz et al. (1980) found declines in 'fluid' intelligence with age. This is a concept proposed by Cattell who suggested that 'crystallised' intelligence comes from experience (and this would be more retained by the elderly), whereas 'fluid' intelligence is related to an abstract problem-solving ability. Baltes and Baltes (1990) found that crystallised intelligence may actually increase with age.

> **Examiner's comment**
> This paragraph describes some **relevant** studies in **good detail** and refers to theories relating to possible changes in IQ. There is an element of **commentary embedded** in this paragraph as a distinction is made between **types** of intelligence.

There are two important considerations. First, these are generalisations and Schultz et al. actually found that some older participants had the highest IQs of all. Second is the cohort effect. When Burns (1966) tested the same individuals at age 22 and again at age 56 their IQs had increased. The data collected by Wechsler was cross-sectional – it compared people aged 20 with people aged 60. When the 60-year-olds were 20 their IQs may have been lower than Wechsler's 20-year-olds because of poorer diets and a lower level of education. The effect was due to the cohort and not declines in old age.

> **Examiner's comment**
> The whole paragraph provides some **useful evaluation** of the research on IQ. It is **succinct yet coherently elaborated.**

Memory is another aspect of cognitive behaviour. Many older people believe they lose their memory. This is supported in a study by Talland (1968) who found that younger participants (20–25-year-olds) were able to remember twice as many items on a short-term memory test than older participants (aged over 75). However, it may well be that this kind of finding applies rather specifically to laboratory studies of memory and that older people are actually quite competent in everyday life, especially when they are motivated to be so. Other research has shown that long-term recall and expert memory skills are retained.

Other research has considered mental processing speeds. It appears that older people do less well on tasks requiring speed of processing, but Stuart-Hamilton (2000) suggests that slower processing times could be explained in terms of having to think through more options as a result of having more knowledge. This means that an older person might arrive at a solution more slowly – but it might be a better solution.

In general there are a number of problems in assessing any cognitive changes in old age. First of all, the abilities of some older people may be affected by undetected physical illnesses such as mild strokes. This was found by Birren et al. (1963) who examined men over the age of 65 and found that even though they had no obvious symptoms, on closer examination they did have some conditions that would have affected their performance. A second issue is the effects of institutionalisation. Where older people are living in an institution lack of stimulation may affect them as it does younger children. This would explain decline in performance in terms of situational rather than dispositional factors. Rubin (1973) found that elderly people living in their own homes performed better on Piagetian tasks than those living in institutions. Havighurst's activity theory suggests that it is important for adults to remain active in later life to maintain psychological health.

A further issue worth considering is the culturally specific nature of these observations. In many cultures the old are revered for their wisdom. It may be only Western society who suspect older people become less able cognitively and ignore the other cognitive skills they have to offer. Arlin (1977) suggested that there is a fifth stage in cognitive development: divergent thinking and problem-finding, and this appears as one gets older.

In our culture where there are very negative stereotypes of the elderly this may have a self-fulfilling effect on their performance. Levy and Langer (1994) supported this in a study looking at profoundly deaf and 'normal' elderly, finding that the deaf individuals did better on memory tasks and also held more positive stereotypes of old people. It could be that the deaf individuals were less exposed to negative stereotypes and this would explain their different stereotypes and their better performance. The conclusion must be that you should believe you can do anything no matter how old you are!

5 Comparative Psychology

How to score full marks

Language is dependent on such complex cognitive and anatomical features that at first it seems to be the exception to the otherwise clear pattern of continuity between humans and other primates. Beginning in the 1960s, a series of projects has documented the behaviour of chimpanzees (e.g. Savage-Rumbaugh 1986) and marine mammals (Schusterman 1989) that have been trained to respond to American Sign

Language or to arbitrary symbols. A second approach has been to focus on the natural communicative systems of non-human animals. A major goal of this approach is to determine whether the signals used by other species have evolved properties in common with human language. Research in this area has searched for three types of cognitive ability. Firstly, it has considered whether the animals, like humans, are able to partition the structure of sounds into discrete categories. Secondly, it has investigated whether animal signals can be considered to describe external objects or environmental events. Thirdly, research has investigated whether the production of animal signals shows a sensitivity to the presence of appropriate receivers. Research in these three areas has revealed that the parallels between animal communication and human language are more extensive than is commonly supposed.

> **Examiner's comment**
> This is a clever first paragraph because it gives an **overview** of research in the area **without getting bogged down in the descriptive details** of all the different studies. The material refers to **appropriate studies** (e.g. Savage-Rumbaugh, Schusterman), but **summarises** their findings in an **effective and discursive** way.

Further parallels between animal communication and language are suggested by studies of song learning in birds, which reveal the existence of a sensitive period early in life and the importance of auditory feedback (Marler 1991). Song learning thus provides evidence of the language criterion of 'traditional transmission' – transmission from one generation to the next (Hockett 1960). This vocal learning process also gives rise to geographical variation in structure which is the equivalent of to linguistic dialects. Production of learned song, like human speech, is controlled by distinct regions on one side of the brain. Research with primates, especially the Japanese macaque, has shown an enhanced ability to discriminate species-specific calls when they are presented to the right ear (and hence the left hemisphere). In some species, there is also evidence of 'turn-taking', reminiscent of that which occurs during conversations, suggesting that there are rules determining when the production of a signal is appropriate (Chaiken 1990).

> **Examiner's comment**
> As with the first paragraph, this second one **continues to offer an overview of research** into 'natural' animal language. We are told of research that has demonstrated the importance of vocal learning in songbirds, and of geographical variations that are 'the equivalent of linguistic dialects' in humans. Language is mainly located in the left hemisphere of the human brain, so it supports the claim for the same skill in non-human primates that such specialisation is also evident in Japanese macaques. This paragraph is **packed full of important content** which is also compared with Hockett's 'design features' of language as a way of clarifying its status as 'language' rather than simply 'communication'.

Although these parallels between the properties of animal communication and those of human language are extensive, there are no animal signal systems that have all the characteristics just described. There is, for example, no evidence of vocal learning in non-human primates. Animal calls that have been so far studied appear to provide information about the approach of potential predators (Seyfarth and Cheney 1980) or the discovery of food. There is no evidence, however, that animals are capable of describing abstract concepts (such as 'right' or 'wrong'), nor evidence that animal calls have anything that corresponds to the grammatical items (e.g. of, and, which) which allow humans to encode information about relative properties such as size, position and number, as well as indicating tense.

The most dramatic contrast between animal communication and human language is provided by syntax. Many animal signals superficially resemble sentences, but there is little evidence for the property of 'lexical syntax', i.e. for variation in the order of elements that causes changes in meaning. For example, 'the dog chased the cat' has a very different meaning from 'the cat chased the dog', but there is little or no evidence that such syntactical rules appear in non-human communication. The rule-based nature of syntax gives rise to the property of 'productivity', the ability to generate an essentially infinite variety of meaningful new utterances using a relatively small set of basic components. Despite the extraordinary flexibility conferred by productivity, studies of animal signals provide no evidence of the evolution of such an ability in non-human animals.

6 Perspectives: Individual Differences

🎯 How to score full marks

One way to explain schizophrenia, as the quotation suggests, is in terms of genetic influences. There are several sources of genetic evidence. First, twin studies are used to conduct natural experiments comparing the effects of genes with the effects of environment. Gottesman and Shields (1982) used the Maudsley twin register and found 58% concordance for MZ twins reared apart (to ensure that environment could not explain any similarity). Cardo et al. (1999) found 40% concordance in MZ twins compared with 5% in DZ twins. This shows that genetic influences are important though the samples are often quite small and distinguishing between MZ and DZ twins is not always reliable.

A second line of evidence for genetic influence comes from adoption studies. For example, the Finnish adoption study has followed two groups of children from an early age. 7% of those whose mothers had been diagnosed as schizophrenic developed the disorder compared with 1.5% of a control group. We must always consider the possibility that diagnosis is not reliable – some of the mothers initially labelled 'schizophrenic' may have actually been suffering from a different disorder.

A third approach is gene mapping where an attempt is made to identify a particular gene present in individuals with schizophrenia. Sherrington et al. (1988) found evidence for a cluster of genes on chromosome 5, which might make an individual susceptible. Subsequent studies have not confirmed this.

Finally, a very useful approach is to look at high-risk studies where individuals who are identified as high risk because one or both parents have schizophrenia are followed through childhood. In the Israeli high-risk study, at a 13-year follow up 16 out of 50 offspring had been diagnosed as schizophrenic as compared to 4 out of 50 from a control group. This appears to be quite strong evidence for a genetic component, however we can see that by no means all or even half of such children go on to develop the disorder. It is also possible that we can explain this correlation as being due to being brought up by a disturbed parent.

> **Examiner's comment**
> This is an example of **concurrent evaluation**. Each explanation is offered and followed immediately with some comment and/or evaluation to gain both AO1 and AO2 credit. The candidate has provided evidence of synopticity through the use of **different sources of evidence** and **different approaches to evaluation**.

A key point is that studies of genetic influences never show anything like 100% concordance. Therefore we can see that there must be other influences as well. One possibility is to look at other biological explanations. A strong contender is the dopamine hypothesis. The possible involvement of dopamine was suggested by the success of those drugs that reduce the symptoms of schizophrenia and which were found to inhibit dopamine activity. It was also noted that L-dopa (which increases dopamine activity) leads to schizophrenic-like symptoms in 'normal' individuals. This has been confirmed in studies using PET scans (e.g. Wong et al.) where dopamine receptor sites have been found to be denser in schizophrenics. However this has not been replicated.

The main drawback to the dopamine hypothesis is that we cannot know for certain whether such activity is a cause of the disorder or an effect. Nevertheless the dopamine hypothesis is linked to a successful form of treatment and this is the main drive behind trying to find a successful explanation.

> **Examiner's comment**
> This paragraph begins well with a reference to the quotation again, tying the essay to the quotation as is required by the question set. The dopamine hypothesis is clearly explained (AO1), analysed and assessed (AO2).

A more recent development has been to look at evolutionary explanations (which are also biological). Stevens and Price (1996) have proposed the group splitting hypothesis suggesting that when social groups become too big they are more at risk from predation and have more difficulty with food. A 'crazy' individual may act as a leader and enable one subgroup to split off from a main group. This would mean that certain schizophrenic traits (e.g. bizarre beliefs, delusions) serve an adaptive function under certain conditions and that's why the gene for the disorder persists. Such explanations have consequences for the treatment of mental disorder as evolutionary psychiatrists argue that it is more useful to understand the function of a disorder, which may then lead you to the root of the problem than just being able to describe the symptoms.

One difficulty with biological explanations is that they are highly determinist. In other words, they suggest that one's future is largely fixed by one's biology, though as we have seen the evidence doesn't support the full determinist view.

In contrast to these genetic and other biological explanations there are those explanations for schizophrenia which are grouped together as psychological. There are many of these such as Freud's formulation or the social drift hypothesis. Perhaps the most memorable one is Bateson's double-bind hypothesis. Bateson et al. (1956) suggested that some parents send conflicting messages to their children and this leads to confusion, self-doubt and eventual withdrawal. This hypothesis can account for the confused thinking of schizophrenic patients. However, it suffers from the serious problem that there is very little evidence supporting it. There are other theories which point to family interactions as being important such as the idea of a schizophrenogenic mother or the concept of expressed emotion in families.

The diathesis-stress model offers a way to combine the various explanations. This suggests that some individuals are genetically predisposed to schizophrenia but only when certain environmental triggers are additionally present does schizophrenia actually develop. Such triggers might be certain stressful life experiences or living in a family with high expressed emotion. This was supported by the Finnish adoption study which found that all those high-risk children who did develop schizophrenia came from families classified as 'disturbed'. In addition, Day et al. (1987) found that schizophrenics in several countries did tend to experience a high number of stressful life events in the few weeks before the onset of schizophrenia.

7 Perspectives: Issues

How to score full marks

Part of the responsibility of the psychological investigator is to recognise that all research is a social process, carried out in a number of social contexts, each of which has its own norms and cultural expectations. Truly ethical research requires an awareness of and sensitivity to all the social, psychological and cultural contexts in which research might take place, and an awareness of the potential for stereotyping and other biases (e.g., white middle-class heterosexual biases) that might influence the research process. Some areas of research are particularly sensitive in that they are concerned with aspects of behaviour (e.g. drug taking, abnormal behaviour) or areas of the population (e.g. homosexuals, the elderly or the disabled) for which there may be significant consequences as a result of the research.

There are always some social consequences to participation in research but there is also the potential for a more indirect impact on the participant's family, their co-workers, or maybe even the group that the participant represents (e.g. women, the elderly and so on). It does not seem sufficient, therefore, to simply safeguard the interests of the individual in research, there must also be some consideration of the likely impact of the research on the larger group of which the participant is a member. As a result of this need to consider the wider issues of research, some professional bodies (such as the Canadian Psychological Association) advise that all those likely to be affected by the research must be considered when making ethical decisions.

Some of the negative consequences of psychological research may actually further disadvantage groups who may already be disadvantaged (the elderly or the disabled). The CPA advises consultation with members of these groups to consider the appropriateness of the research questions and the research methods, the interpretation of results and of any recommendations that may arise from the research. The advantage of this approach not only demonstrates respect for potential participants but it may also enhance the validity of the research, increasing its relevance to the group or groups concerned. A further consideration is who should be 'allowed' to carry out research with whom. The implication here is, for example, that only male homosexuals should be allowed to conduct research with other male homosexuals, and that a female heterosexual psychologist would not have sufficient empathy to ask relevant questions to this particular group of participants.

One of the feminist criticisms of psychology with respect to its representation of women has been that, traditionally, researchers have studied women's behaviour in the artificial context of the psychological laboratory. This 'decontextualisation' of women's lives by researchers affects the validity of the results and, as a consequence, may deny women the benefits that might arise from accurate research. It is, therefore, both a scientific issue *and* an ethical issue. Nicolson (1995) points out that much of the scientific research into, for example, the effects of menstruation or PMS has served to 'pathologise' women's behaviour purely in terms of their bodies. One of the sources of inaccuracy in some areas of research has been the tendency to consider males as the norm and females as somehow a deviation from the norm. This bias can result in inappropriate interpretations of results that serve to disadvantage women even further.

Many other groups in society have suffered the consequences of having been excluded from research or being misrepresented when they have been included. It might be argued that our understanding of human behaviour has been lessened by our misinterpretations of, or our failure to include, representative samples of persons with disabilities, the elderly, the disadvantaged, and members of minority cultures. It follows, then, that a redressing of these imbalances in research can improve the quality of psychological research in these areas. The failure to accurately represent and research such groups carries with it an additional ethical issue, the fact that these groups then miss out on any of the potential benefits of such research.

Psychologists typically deal with ethical issues in research by the development of strict guidelines for the conduct of their studies. Ethical guidelines may protect the immediate needs of research participants, but may not deal with all the possible ways in which research may inflict harm on a group of people or section of society. However, some of the controversies that arise from socially sensitive research can be attributed to poorly designed or executed studies or inappropriate interpretations of the findings. Although other scientists may be aware of these problems (and therefore be aware of the limitations of the research and its conclusions), the media and the public may not, and thus poor studies might shape important social policy to the detriment of those groups represented by the research.

8 Perspectives: Debates

🎯 How to score full marks

A balanced argument would be to consider in what ways Psychology can be considered to be a science and also to examine the alternative view, that it is not a science. Before we can begin to answer this question we need to establish what we mean when we attempt to assess whether a subject is a science.

The scientific tradition, as established by logical positivists, emphasises objectivity and replicability. The aim of science was and is to collect observations which are unbiased by the person making the observations. The aim is also to conduct research that can be replicated. Only in this way can the validity of results be confirmed. For example, if you repeated a study conducted by someone else and did not produce the same findings then this throws the original findings into doubt. This has been done with many well-known experiments. For example, Milgram's classic obedience research has been repeated in many different cultural settings and reported to produce similar results – though there is some doubt about whether the same procedures were followed or whether the methodology had the same meaning in other cultures.

A further aspect of science is the use of the scientific method – by this we do not mean solely the use of experiments but adhering to the stages of making precise observations, forming theories that explain the observations, generating hypotheses from the theory, testing the hypothesis and using the findings to revise the theory. A good example of this is Latané and Darley's observations of the Kitty Genovese case. Her murder led them to formulate some possible explanations for why help had not been forthcoming, one of which was 'bystander behaviour' (the more people there are the less that help will be forthcoming). They then tested their hypothesis in an experiment where students discussed things over an intercom. There was one real participant who was more quick to offer help when she thought she was alone with one other.

This is an example of a laboratory experiment, the ideal form of scientific study because it is possible to control all variables so that we can be fairly certain that the only variable affecting the dependent variable was the independent variable. This means that we can claim to have demonstrated a cause and an effect.

> **Examiner's comment**
> This segment of the essay has used an example to illustrate how the scientific method is used in Psychology, clearly demonstrating that this is what happens (i.e. showing that Psychology is scientific). The one example given has been provided in **detail,** which is valuable, but there might have been further reference to different **kinds** of methodology in Psychology (observational studies or interviews) which also are conducted along the lines of the scientific method. This wider analysis would have been helpful for greater synopticity.

Psychology is defined as the *scientific* study of behaviour and experience, in order to emphasise its aim to be objective and to produce well-controlled replicable experiments. It is also important to draw this distinction in order to differentiate psychological arguments from commonsense ones. The distinction lies in the collection of objective and verifiable facts which lead to the formulation of empirically based theories.

Clearly then Psychology can claim to be a science because it uses the scientific method for conducting research (as contrasted with, say, Philosophy, which uses rational rather than empirical methods to discover 'facts' about the world). On the other hand, others argue that psychological research is riddled with biases which threaten the validity of the studies. For example, in Asch's conformity study the results have been challenged because they can be explained in terms of demand characteristics – the response of participants to certain cues. Milgram's research has also been challenged because it is claimed it lacked mundane realism and this meant that participants weren't behaving as they would normally behave. The best example of bias in experiments is experimenter bias as demonstrated by Rosenthal and Fode in their study of rats. The student participants were told some rats would learn more quickly than others (even though there was no difference) and these rats did in fact perform better – presumably because the students' expectations affected their performance. In most experimental settings experimenters unwittingly communicate their expectations to participants and participants seek cues about how they should be behaving to help the experimenter.

> **Examiner's comment**
> In this part of the essay the candidate is now looking at the **reverse** arguments, and again making reference to some obvious but useful examples of research where there was bias and also psychological research which may be unbiased but lack validity all the same (i.e. Milgram's study). It might have been helpful to make the **distinction** between these two points clearer. The Rosenthal and Fode study is an example again of bias. Note that dates have not been included; the candidate would not be penalised for this. Names and dates add detail to your answers and may be useful if considering the historical (cultural) setting of the research, as in the case of some conformity research, which was conducted in the United States in the 1950s when conformity was very high, and anti-conformity was frowned upon.

However, bias isn't restricted to psychological research. There are problems of bias in even the physical sciences. Heisenberg (1927) claimed that simply the act of making an observation changes the observation, thus no objective research is ever possible. This issue becomes more problematic in psychology where the object of study is active and intelligent.

> **Examiner's comment**
> It might be useful to say what we can **conclude** from this (and thereby adding some AO2 commentary). For example, the candidate might have added 'this shows that the problem of bias exists in all sciences and not just psychology, so bias alone should not be grounds for excluding psychology'.

Kuhn (1970) suggested that psychology has not yet evolved into a science because there is no single paradigm or perspective which encompasses all of human behaviour research. Though others such as Palermo (1971) argued that, far from being a prescience, psychology has already undergone several paradigm shifts, such as behaviourism and the information-processing paradigm. Palermo suggests that psychology is in fact now in the revolution phase.

On balance the arguments suggest that Psychology can claim to be as much a science as any other science. But there is a further issue. This is the question about whether the goals of science are actually appropriate to psychology. The scientific approach is both determinist and reductionist because (a) it seeks to demonstrate causal (deterministic) relationships and (b) it reduces complex behaviours to operationally defined variables for the purpose of research (experimental reductionism). The end result is that the behaviour psychologists study in scientific experiments may lack ecological validity, i.e. the results will not generalise to real life. For example, studies of memory have tended to focus on a particular sort of memory (recall for word lists) that can be well controlled. This only represents some aspects of memory. Other aspects, such as skills, are harder to study in this reductionist way.

> **Examiner's comment**
> It is useful to bring in a different area of psychology (memory rather than the social psychology mentioned so far) to increase the linkages across the specification. It is also creditworthy that the candidate has **elaborated** the point about memory rather than simply saying 'for example, memory research'.

A further problem with all research in psychology (not just experiments) is that it is inevitably based on restricted samples, in psychology these are culturally and socially biased, producing theories which are not universally valid and therefore can't be generalised. For example, Sears showed that a large percentage of psychological studies are based on white American college students. Such participants are atypical in many ways and it is actually quite frightening to think that many psychological theories are actually derived from this sample.

> **Examiner's comment**
> It is legitimate to express what may seem to be 'personal opinion' ('it is quite frightening') as long as this is a **psychologically informed** opinion.

Humanistic psychologists such as Harré (1979) feel that objective data can tell us little about subjective experience. It has statistical but not human meaning. New research methods are needed to properly investigate human behaviour, for example social constructionists challenge the notion of a physical reality and suggest that the reality that we construct socially is more relevant. More subjective methods of research can be validated through, for example, triangulation. Triangulation is achieved by comparing the findings from a number of different studies or using different methods within one study. Close agreement confirms the validity of the findings and this produces relatively objective data. This means that we end up with a kind of research that is more valid and yet also objective. It is a move away from the positivist approach to science, and one that might promise more for an understanding of human behaviour.

> **Examiner's comment**
> The discussion of different methodologies is useful evidence of synopticity. It is also a neat way to end the essay by considering the fact that other research methods might still be counted as 'scientific' despite not being in the tradition of logical positivism which sought to demonstrate determinist relationships.

9 Perspectives: Approaches

🎯 How to score full marks

(a) Social psychologists might explain Matt's involvement with computer games by focusing on the opportunities that such game playing offers for his social needs. Matt may prefer to play computer games when other positive social activities are not possible. By playing strategy games he also gains the advantage of being able to discuss strategies with other game players, thus giving him the promise of communication with others and overcoming his loneliness. It is also possible that Matt is insecure or in some other way socially inhibited. By playing strategy games over the Internet, where nobody knows who he really is, Matt can be more outgoing than might be possible in real life.

Physiological psychologists might focus more on Matt's addictive behaviour. If he plays for long periods of time it is possible that his computer games act in a similar rewarding way as some addictive drugs. Many activities that give people a natural 'high' cause an increase in the activity of the chemical dopamine in the brain. This sets up a brain reward system so that Matt is motivated to repeat the experience as often as possible. Playing actually makes the brain more efficient at glucose metabolism, therefore although the games may be extremely demanding, the brains of regular players such as Matt deal with their demands more efficiently than the brain of the non- or occasional player.

> **Examiner's comment**
> These two explanations are **clearly focused** on Matt's behaviour as specified by the question. Much of the first explanation is speculative (Matt may just play them because he likes them) but this is the sort of explanation that social psychologists would offer for such behaviour. The emphasis would then be on the testing of these hypotheses. The second explanation does offer some specialist knowledge of addictive behaviour, but it does show that if you are lucky enough to **know** something about the area, grab the chance to use it!

(b) A strength of a physiological explanation of Matt's behaviour is that it can be tested scientifically. This elevates it from being just speculation and means that precise measurements can be taken and any relationship can be clearly demonstrated. Another strength is that such explanations may be used to support the view that Matt is actually doing something useful rather than wasting his time as his parents seem to think. A limitation of physiological explanations is that they are reductionist, and therefore other reasons for Matt's behaviour (such as those suggested in the social psychological explanation) might be overlooked. Another problem is the issue of causation. This explanation assumes that dopamine activity rises as a result of playing computer games, although the reason for this change may have more to do with the social nature of the activity rather than the game itself.

> **Examiner's comment**
> Both strengths and limitations are addressed and in equal detail. Both are **accurate** and clearly expressed **and focused explicitly on Matt's behaviour.** There is a temptation to forget about the stimulus material but this hasn't happened here.

(c) A physiological psychologist might carry out a laboratory experiment to test the hypothesis that playing strategy games (the independent variable) raises levels of dopamine activity in the brain (the dependent variable). They may inject experimental group participants with a tracer chemical that would monitor levels of dopamine activity via a PET (Positron Emission Tomography) scanner. By having one group of participants play a computer game for an hour and have a matched control group stare at a blank screen for the same period, it should be possible to investigate whether dopamine levels increase in the former group compared to the latter.

> **Examiner's comment**
> The laboratory experiment proposed here, although somewhat ambitious, is clearly an **appropriate** way of testing this hypothesis. The independent variable and dependent variable are both **clearly** identified, and although the process of matching could have been explained more, there is a time limit in this question and there are more useful things to say. The use of a PET scanner is an appropriate technique in this context.

(d) By using a control group that does not play computer games it is possible to establish cause and effect – whether it is the actual game play that causes the increase in dopamine levels. Another advantage is that researchers can control other possible extraneous variables such as the time participants spend playing games and any environmental factors such as background noise. However, it is not possible to control all extraneous variables, and in this case some participants may be less successful during game play than others and therefore they find the experience less rewarding. Such experiments also have ethical problems, not least of which is the need for intrusive injection and recording techniques. Participants are usually paid for taking part in such experiments. This may make the situation less realistic for the games players, and any rise in dopamine levels may be due to the lure of the money than the effect of the game.

> **Examiner's comment**
> This answer has included a number of **accurate advantages and disadvantages** of the chosen investigative method. The answer covers the ability to detect cause and effect, the control of variables, ethical issues and problems of validity. What is equally important is that these are **focused on the actual problem** being discussed rather than being a general evaluation of the laboratory method.